Taste favourites

A catalogue record for this book is available from the National Library of New Zealand

A RANDOM HOUSE BOOK
published by
Random House New Zealand
18 Poland Road, Glenfield, Auckland,
New Zealand

www.randomhouse.co.nz

First published 2006

© 2006 Allyson Gofton, Jennifer Yee, Laurie Black, Tracey Sunderland and ACP Media.

The moral rights of the authors have been asserted.

ISBN 13: 978 1 86941 838 0
ISBN 10: 1 86941 838 7

This book is copyright. Except for the purposes of fair reviewing no part of this publication may be reproduced or transmitted in any form or by any means, olectronic or mechanical, including photocopying, recording or any information storage and retrieval system, without permission in writing from the publisher.

Design: Trevor Newman
Printed in China

Taste favourites

Allyson Gofton
Jennifer Yee
Laurie Black
Tracey Sunderland

Photography by:
Aaron McLean
Alan Gillard
Kieran Scott

RANDOM HOUSE
NEW ZEALAND

contents

introduction	6
what's for lunch?	8
midweek meals	32
entertaining	78
food for drinks	96
baking	118
desserts	148
glossary	172
index	174
author profiles	176

introduction

When *Taste* was launched in August 2005 we aimed to deliver an accessible magazine that could be used on a daily basis, with recipes that didn't take too long to prepare and which were made from readily available ingredients. We aim to deliver the same in this, our very first cookbook. As the title implies, it is compiled from favourite *Taste* recipes and it's broken down into occasion-based chapters, just like the magazine. Because primarily we offer speedy but delicious midweek meals you'll find this chapter definitely takes centre stage here. However, on weekends or for special occasions, it can be fun to spend a little longer in the kitchen and so in this book you'll find sections on desserts, baking, nibbles for drinks, entertaining and lunch.

Taste food writers Allyson Gofton, Laurie Black, Jennifer Yee and Tracey Sunderland have all provided scrumptious recipes with enticing photographs from Kieran Scott, Aaron McLean and Alan Gillard. Where applicable, recipes come with variations and cook's tips to make life even easier!

For the *Taste* reader we hope this collection keeps your best-loved tried-and-true recipes quickly at hand as well as providing an introduction for those of you who have not yet caught up with the magazine.

Lastly, while we think this book is as good looking as it is useful, we have not set out to create a coffee table tome. Instead, we hope *Taste Favourites* will become a well-loved cook's companion with plenty to inspire you, your family and friends.

Suzanne Dale
Editor
Taste magazine

Taste
what's for lunch?

I like to pop this into a work or school lunchbox as part of a handy midweek lunch.

TRACEY SUNDERLAND

Baked savoury cheesecake

READY IN: 60 MINUTES
SERVES: 4–6

1½ cups self-raising flour
1 cup red onion, chopped
1½ cups zucchini, grated
1½ cups kumara, grated
1½ cups tasty cheese, grated
½ tsp salt
¼ tsp white pepper
3 eggs, lightly beaten
1 cup blue-top milk
½ cup olive oil
½ cup feta, crumbled
tomato chutney, to serve

1 Sift the flour into a large bowl. Add the onion, grated vegetables and the tasty cheese and season with salt and pepper. Stir well with a fork.
2 Make a well in the centre and add eggs. Pour in milk and oil. Stir the wet mix into the dry mix until it is the consistency of a batter or pikelet mix.
3 Pour the mixture into a greased 22cm square cake tin. Sprinkle the feta over and bake in an oven preheated to 180°C for 35–40 minutes. The cake will rise and show small cracks when ready. Remove from the oven and place tin onto a cooling rack.
4 Once the cheesecake has cooled, remove it from the tin by turning it upside down on to a plate or small board. Wrap in plastic wrap and place in the fridge overnight. To serve, cut into 4 or 6 even-sized pieces. Wrap in paper and package up with little containers of tomato chutney to go.

COOK'S TIPS
• Replace the kumara with sliced raw bacon or smoked chicken to add more protein for growing kids.
• Variations might include grated pumpkin and chopped spinach leaves, or a mix of blue cheese and colby or edam cheese.
• Cut cherry tomatoes in half and place on top before sprinkling with feta.
• A medium-sized zucchini or kumara, grated, measures 1 cup.

These pies can be frozen and make an ideal midweek lunch. Use bought pastry or make your own samosa pastry.

TRACEY SUNDERLAND

Curry puff pies

READY IN: 65 MINUTES
MAKES: 10 PIES

500g medium potatoes, skin on
4 Tbsp canola or soya oil
1 tsp black mustard seeds, optional
1 onion, finely diced
1 Tbsp fresh ginger, finely grated
2-3 tsp curry powder
½ tsp salt
2 Tbsp fresh coriander, chopped, optional
2 Tbsp lemon juice
250g minced lamb
5 pre-rolled sheets savoury short pastry (800g)
3 Tbsp soya oil

Samosa pastry, optional (see step 6)
300g flour
½ tsp salt
4 Tbsp oil
4 Tbsp water

1 Boil the potatoes in salted water for 10 minutes until just tender. Allow to cool for 5 minutes in cold water then drain, peel and cut into a 1cm dice.
2 Heat 2 Tbsp of the oil in a frying pan and fry mustard seeds until they begin to pop. Add onion and ginger and cook for about 3-4 minutes, stirring as you go. Add curry powder and salt and cook for 1 minute. Add the diced potato and cook for 2-3 minutes until the potatoes have absorbed the flavour. Remove from the heat and add the coriander and lemon juice. Stir well and add extra salt to taste, then transfer to a flat tray and leave to cool.
3 Rinse the pan out then reheat, adding 2 Tbsp of oil. Fry the minced lamb until separated and browned. Remove from the heat and add to the plate of spiced potatoes and mix well with a fork.
4 Using a rolling pin, lightly roll out a pastry sheet until the edges cover the plastic underneath. Using a dinner plate turned upside down, cut out 1 round. The pastry circle needs to be as large as the square of pastry. Cut the round in half, take one half and brush the edges with water. Place ½ cup of filling in the centre and fold the pastry in half to enclose the filling. Press the straight edges together and crimp the other end with your fingertips to seal. Repeat until you have 10 pies.
5 Brush the pies with oil, sprinkle with salt, place on an oven tray and bake at 220°C for 20 minutes. Leave to cool then cover and chill.
6 To make samosa pastry, sift the flour with the salt into a bowl and make a well in the centre. Mix together the oil and water and gradually add this to the flour to make a firm dough. Knead for 5 minutes until smooth. Cover and rest for 30-40 minutes before rolling out.

Perk up your lunch break with a quick homemade salad. Sometimes I serve this to friends for a casual dinner. It's something that can be made well in advance.

TRACEY SUNDERLAND

Chicken noodle salad

READY IN: 35 MINUTES
SERVES: 4

Salad
2 chicken breasts, or 4 pieces on the bone, cooked
2 x 220g packets Kan Tong Express Hokkien noodles
1 Tbsp oil
2 carrots, cut into sticks
1 yellow pepper, cut into sticks
100g snow peas
2 cups broccoli florets
2 cups cherry tomatoes
1 cup mung bean sprouts

Dressing
¼ cup light soy sauce
¼ cup honey, warmed
¼ cup oyster sauce
¼ cup olive oil
2 Tbsp lemon juice
¼ cup toasted sesame seeds, for sprinkling

1 Pull the cooked chicken apart into small pieces. Remove any bones and place chicken in a large bowl.
2 Cook the noodles by snipping off one end of the packet and microwaving for 45 seconds. Tip out into a colander. Alternatively, add noodles to boiling water for 1 minute then drain in a colander. Cool by pouring cold tap water over the colander for 30 seconds or so. Shake out water then pour 1 Tbsp oil over and toss through the noodles. Add noodles to the chicken.
3 Blanch carrots, pepper, snow peas and broccoli in boiling water for 1 minute and refresh in iced water. Vegetables should be crisp and only partly cooked. Add blanched vegetables, cherry tomatoes and bean sprouts to the bowl of chicken and noodles.
4 Pour all dressing ingredients into a jar. Cover and shake well to mix. Pour over the salad and toss through with your hands.
5 Tip into 4 lunchboxes. Sprinkle with toasted sesame seeds. Pack with a disposable fork.

COOK'S TIPS
• Try changing the noodles — use udon noodles and add different meats, such as leftover pieces of barbecued steak cut into slices.
• Instead of chicken, you could use seafood, such as grilled squid, which can be marinated in the dressing with a little chilli paste or fresh garlic. Then top with toasted cashew nuts for a more exotic look.

Adding lots of spinach at the end gives the green velvet soup its emerald colour, while split dried peas create the velvety texture.

LAURIE BLACK

Green velvet soup

READY IN: 1 HOUR 30 MINUTES
MAKES: 8 BOWLS OR 1.8 LITRES

1 onion, diced
1 celery stick, sliced
1 large floury potato (Agria or Ilam Hardy), peeled and cut in chunks
½ cup split green peas
2 bay leaves
3 cups vegetable stock
2½ cups water
1 head broccoli, stem discarded and remainder chopped
2 colanders washed spinach leaves
1½ cups basil leaves
½ lemon, juiced

1 Put onion, celery, potato, split peas, bay leaves, stock and water in a large saucepan and bring to the boil. Cover and simmer for 1 hour until split peas are very tender.
2 Add broccoli, cover again and simmer for 10 minutes.
3 Add spinach and basil, stirring just until the spinach has wilted.
4 Remove from heat and discard bay leaves. Using a stick blender, food processor or blender, purée the soup until smooth. Season to taste.
5 Reheat soup before serving (or just before pouring into thermos flasks), remove from heat and add lemon juice.

This potato cream soup is ideal to pop into a thermos flask to take along on a winter picnic. The goat's feta & smoked bacon sandwiches are just the thing to have with it.

LAURIE BLACK

Potato cream soup

READY IN: 50 MINUTES
MAKES: 6 BOWLS OR 1.3 LITRES

- 1 Tbsp light olive oil
- 1 knob butter
- 1 medium onion, sliced
- 1 leek, sliced (white part only)
- 2 cloves garlic, crushed
- 1 bay leaf
- 1 tsp salt
- 3 large floury potatoes (Agria or Ilam Hardy), peeled and chunked
- 2 cups chicken stock
- 1 cup water
- 200ml cream

1 Heat oil and butter in large saucepan just until butter melts. Add onion, leek, garlic, bay leaf and salt, and cook gently with the lid on until the onion is soft but not coloured. Stir occasionally.
2 Add potato and stir to combine. Add stock and water, then just bring to the boil, cover and simmer for 20–30 minutes until the potato is very tender.
3 Remove from the heat and discard the bay leaf. Using a stick blender, food processor or blender, purée the soup until smooth. Season to taste.
4 Reheat the soup to serve. Do not boil again after cream has been added.

Goat's feta & smoked bacon brown bread sandwiches

READY IN: 5–10 MINUTES
SERVES: 8

- 100g goat's feta
- 2 Tbsp yoghurt
- 2 rashers smoked bacon, cut in strips
- 1 tsp vegetable oil
- 16 thin slices crusty brown bread

1 Blend feta and yoghurt until smooth. Refrigerate for at least one hour, or until required.
2 Fry bacon in oil until nice and crisp. Drain on kitchen paper.
3 Spread feta mixture on 8 slices of bread, scatter bacon on top and cover with a second slice.

Whether you're painting the house or just shunting stuff around, the ring-ins on your working bee surely deserve some nourishing treats. These pita sandwiches are ideal.

LAURIE BLACK

Pita filled with grilled eggplant, yoghurt, dukkah & coriander

READY: OVERNIGHT
SERVES: 4

1½ cups thick yoghurt
½ eggplant, sliced crosswise into 1.5cm-thick half-circles
olive oil
4 medium-sized pita rounds
2 Tbsp dukkah (see Glossary, page 172)
½ cup coriander leaves

1 Line a colander or large sieve with a double layer of kitchen paper towels and place over a bowl. Tip in the yoghurt and cover with plastic wrap to seal. Leave to drain in the fridge overnight. Discard whey from the bowl in the morning and transfer thickened yoghurt to a small bowl.
2 Heat a baking sheet on the lower rack of a 200°C oven (remove any higher racks for this recipe). Brush eggplant slices liberally with olive oil and place on the hot sheet. Bake for 10–12 minutes then flip each piece over using a thin metal fish slice. Bake for a further 10–12 minutes or until golden brown. Set eggplant slices on a rack to cool.
3 Split each pita bread open carefully. Spread the inside thickly with yoghurt, then add eggplant slices. Sprinkle dukkah into each pita and finish with coriander leaves. Wrap and keep cool until required.

COOK'S TIP
• Straining yoghurt is a good way of making a spreadable, tangy filling for sandwiches. You can also add herbs, garlic and other seasonings and spread it on crackers or croutons to serve with drinks.

A proper frittata is made in a frying pan, but by making it in a baking tray you can use a lot less oil, and it's all ready to take on a picnic as soon as it cools.

LAURIE BLACK

Golden onion & herb frittata

READY IN: 20 MINUTES
SERVES: 6–8

    2 medium onions, peeled and cut in wedges
    1 Tbsp olive oil
    2 cloves garlic, sliced
    8 eggs
    2 Tbsp milk
    1 tsp salt
    freshly ground black pepper
    1 cup of 3 different fresh herbs, such as basil,
       parsley, thyme, chervil, chives, dill

1 Sauté onion in oil until golden brown. Add garlic and cook for 1 minute, then remove from heat and allow to cool.
2 In a large bowl, beat eggs and milk to thoroughly combine. Add salt and pepper, herbs and onion and garlic mixture then stir well to mix.
3 Brush a shallow 18cm × 28cm baking tray with a little more oil. Pour the egg mixture into the pan, making sure the onion and herbs are evenly distributed.
4 Bake at 180°C for 14 minutes until firm. Cool on a rack. Cut into squares to serve.

COOK'S TIP
• For a winter picnic, sneak a little chilli into the food to warm people up.

Served hot or cold, these spicy little meat pies will become a welcome treat for all your family and friends.

LAURIE BLACK

Little lamb pies with rosemary, chilli & tomato

READY IN: 1 HOUR
MAKES: 18 PIES

2 tsp olive oil
2 cloves garlic, crushed
leaves from rosemary sprig, finely chopped
250g lean minced lamb
½ tsp ground chilli powder
½ x 400g tin chopped tomatoes, with juice
½ cup water
¼ tsp salt
4 sheets pre-rolled flaky pastry
a little flour
1 egg yolk, mixed with 1 Tbsp water
tomato chutney, to serve

1 Heat oil with garlic and rosemary in a frying pan until the garlic just starts to sizzle.
2 Increase the heat and quickly add the mince and chilli powder, breaking up the mince as it browns. Stir in tomatoes and juice, water and salt. Reduce heat and simmer for 30 minutes, stirring occasionally. Add plenty of pepper, transfer mince to a bowl and cool.
3 Cut nine 7.5cm-diameter circles from each sheet of pastry. Set half aside, dust the bench with a little flour and roll out remaining circles a little more with a floured rolling pin so their diameter increases slightly. Place 1 Tbsp mince in the middle of each smaller circle. Working with one circle at a time, wet your fingertip with cold water and run it around the edge of the pastry to make a damp ring.
4 Neatly press a larger circle of pastry over the top, pressing the edge down firmly onto the damp circle to seal the pie shut. Crimp the pastry by repeatedly pressing the end of a teaspoon along the edge of the circle. Using a sharp knife, cut a 2cm vent into the lid of each pie. Brush the tops with a little egg yolk and water mixture.
5 Arrange pies on baking sheets covered with baking paper. Bake at 200°C for 15 minutes or until pastry is golden and crisp. Cool on racks. Serve with your favourite chunky tomato chutney — so delicious!

COOK'S TIP
- If you don't like the flavour of lamb, try these using beef.

I ate a similar salad to this at a lovely little neighbourhood bistro in Sydney. It's light, tangy and refreshing.

LAURIE BLACK

Smoked fish, lemon, parsley & celery-heart salad

READY IN: 5 MINUTES
SERVES: 4–6

2 cups flaked smoked fish, such as snapper or kahawai
1 cup flat leaf parsley, roughly torn
pale heart stalks (plus any other little tender stalks) from 1 whole celery, sliced
½ small Meyer lemon, very thinly sliced
2 lemons, juiced
2 Tbsp extra virgin olive oil
½ tsp sea salt

1 Toss everything together in a wide mixing bowl. Season to taste.
2 Serve on a platter.

COOK'S TIP
- Chilled in advance, a thermos with a wide neck is just the thing for transporting a salad. Tip the salad onto a serving plate at lunchtime and nothing will have wilted.

This 25-minute main-course salad is fresh and moreish — perfect for vegetarians, too.

TRACEY SUNDERLAND

Beetroot, apple & blue cheese salad with walnut cider dressing

READY IN: 25 MINUTES
SERVES: 4

Dressing
1 Tbsp Dijon mustard
2 Tbsp cider vinegar
4 Tbsp walnut or almond oil
2 Tbsp olive oil

Salad
250g can whole baby beetroot, drained or fresh cooked beetroot (see Cook's Tip)
4 Braeburn or Pacific rose apples, unpeeled, cut into quarters
2 sticks celery
2 cups radicchio leaves
1 bunch watercress shoots, roots removed
1 green oak lettuce, washed and torn
100g blue cheese, crumbled
½ cup fresh walnuts, toasted
3 Tbsp chives, sliced

1 Put the mustard into a small bowl and whisk in the vinegar. Pour the oils in slowly and whisk to emulsify the dressing. Season to taste.
2 Place the drained beetroot on a plate lined with a paper towel, cover with another piece of paper towel and pat to absorb as much juice as you can. Leave beetroot this way while you prepare the other salad ingredients.
3 Cut the apple quarters into fine slices and place in a large bowl. Cut the celery on an angle into thin slices and add to the apples. Add radicchio, watercress and lettuce leaves. Pour the dressing over the salad mix. Use your hands to toss lightly until the entire salad is coated.
4 Arrange salad mixture on a large platter. Add the baby beetroot and crumble the blue cheese over the top. Add walnuts and sprinkle with sliced chives to serve.

COOK'S TIP
• Cook whole fresh beetroot in a large saucepan covered with cold water. Do not top and tail or they will bleed. Add 1 tsp salt, bring to the boil and cook for 20–25 minutes until tender. Using rubber gloves, peel by removing beetroot from the pan and running them under cold water. The skins will slip off easily.

This flavoursome meal in a bowl makes a great Sunday lunch to share with friends.

LAURIE BLACK

Mexican albondigas soup with limes & soft tortillas

READY IN: 1 HOUR 20 MINUTES
SERVES: 2 AS A MAIN

Meatballs
300g lean beef mince
3 Tbsp long-grain rice
1 egg
¼ cup chopped mint
½ tsp salt
½ tsp freshly ground black pepper

Soup
2 cloves garlic, crushed
1 onion, diced
1 carrot, diced
2 Tbsp chopped coriander stalks
1 Tbsp vegetable oil
½ tsp salt
½ tsp cumin seeds
475g tin chopped tomatoes
½ litre water, or chicken or vegetable stock

To serve
¼ cup coriander leaves
fresh lime
warmed soft tortillas

1 Mix all the meatball ingredients together well. Cover and chill for 30 minutes, or until ready to cook, then roll mixture into even, golfball-sized balls.
2 Add garlic, onion, carrot and coriander stalks to the oil in a large saucepan, sprinkle with the salt and sweat over a low heat until onion is soft.
3 Add cumin seeds and cook for another 2 minutes, then add tomatoes and water, or stock. Bring to the boil, cover, and reduce heat to simmer the soup for 5 minutes.
4 Gently add meatballs to the soup and simmer a further 20–25 minutes, turning meatballs over once, until meatballs are cooked through and the rice is tender. Adjust seasoning to taste.
5 To serve, scatter coriander leaves on top. Accompany with fresh lime to squeeze over and warmed tortillas to the side.

Taste
midweek meals

This is a great way to use leftover Christmas ham, but it will be a hit all year round with ham from the deli.

TRACEY SUNDERLAND

Picnic pie of ham, egg & roasted tomato

READY IN: 55 MINUTES
SERVES: 6

4 tomatoes
2 large onions, peeled and sliced into rings
2 Tbsp olive oil
400g block of flaky puff pastry
 (defrosted overnight in fridge)
3 eggs
¾ cup cream
1 Tbsp Dijon mustard
½ tsp salt
4 slices ham
1 cup tasty cheese, grated
1 Tbsp parsley, chopped
1 Tbsp chives, chopped

1 Cut tomatoes into wedges and remove the core and place on an oven tray. Repeat with the onions on a separate tray. Sprinkle tomatoes and onions with oil and season. Roast in an oven preheated to 200°C for 20 minutes. Remove from the oven and leave in a cool place.
2 Meanwhile, grease a 9.5cm × 33.5cm rectangular springform tin with oil or butter. Cut the pastry block in half, roll out the base evenly to measure approximately 16cm × 40cm. Let the pastry rest for a minute or so before lining the tin. Press the pastry well into each corner, lining the base and the sides of the tin. Leave a little pastry hanging over the sides. There needs to be a little rim of pastry to press the lid onto. Place the lined tin in the fridge for a few minutes to rest.
3 In a bowl, whisk the eggs with the cream, mustard and salt.
4 To make the pie, cover the pastry base with cooked onion. Layer the ham over the onion, then scatter grated cheese, herbs and roasted tomatoes into the dish. Pour over the egg mix and brush the pastry edges well with egg mix.
5 Roll out the remaining pastry into a rectangle measuring 12cm × 35cm. Let the pastry rest for a minute or so and then lay over the pie filling and press the edges together well with your fingertips. With a pastry brush, glaze the pie top with any mix left in the bottom of the egg and cream bowl. Using the tip of a sharp knife, make little pricks in the pastry to let out the air while the pie cooks.
6 Bake at 220°C for 35 minutes or until golden and cooked. Serve hot or cold with a tasty chutney or relish.

Make the most of ham with this tasty lasagne dish. Serve with a salad and some crusty bread for a complete meal.

TRACEY SUNDERLAND

Spinach & ham lasagne

READY IN: 60 MINUTES
SERVES: 4–6

Béchamel sauce
2 Tbsp butter
3 Tbsp flour
pinch of nutmeg
¼ tsp salt
2½ cups milk
2 Tbsp Dijon mustard
1¼ cups tasty cheese, grated
white pepper

Lasagne
2 Tbsp oil
2 cloves garlic, crushed
6 large tomatoes, blanched (see Cook's Tip)
400g packet egg lasagne sheets
8 slices ham
130g packet washed baby spinach leaves

1 To make the béchamel sauce, melt the butter in a saucepan, sprinkle the flour over and stir well. Cook for 2 minutes over a gentle heat. Add nutmeg and salt and stir well. Continue stirring and add the milk slowly, half a cup at a time. Stir until the sauce begins to thicken and is smooth, adding the remaining milk. Allow the sauce to simmer on a low heat for 2 minutes then stir in mustard, 1 cup of the cheese and season with white pepper. Stir well. Simmer for 2 minutes then remove from the heat.
2 Heat a frying pan. Add oil, cook garlic over a low heat for 1 minute. Add roughly diced tomatoes and simmer for 5–6 minutes until the tomatoes have reduced to a thin sauce.
3 To compile the lasagne, grease a deep 22cm × 22cm baking dish. Spread 1 large spoon of tomato sauce over the base of the dish. Cover with a sheet of lasagne, then half the ham. Spoon over half the tomato sauce and arrange half the spinach leaves on top. Drizzle half a ladleful of béchamel sauce over the ingredients, cover with a pasta sheet and repeat. Finish with a sheet of pasta. Cover with remaining béchamel sauce. Sprinkle over remaining grated cheese and bake in an oven preheated to 175°C for 35–40 minutes.

COOK'S TIP
• To blanch tomatoes, cut a cross along the skin at the base. Remove the core. Drop into a pot of boiling water for 8 seconds. The skin will fall away.

This one-pot meal is just what you need on a cool night.
TRACEY SUNDERLAND

Lamb & cashew curry

READY IN: 60 MINUTES
SERVES: 4

600g lamb steaks, cubed
150g natural yoghurt
2 onions, peeled
2 cloves garlic, peeled
1 green chilli, stalk removed
1 Tbsp fresh ginger or 1 tsp dried ginger
2 Tbsp curry powder
100g cashew nuts
2 Tbsp oil

To serve
mint leaves
steamed rice
blanched green beans
roti

1 Put the lamb cubes in a bowl and mix in half the yoghurt. Toss until all the cubes are coated.
2 Put onions, garlic, chilli, ginger, curry powder, cashew nuts and 3–4 Tbsp water into a food processor bowl and process to a smooth paste. Alternatively, finely slice everything, then stir in the water.
3 Heat a heavy-based saucepan, add oil and cook the spice paste over a low heat for 2 minutes. Once the sauce starts to thicken, add the lamb and season well with salt. Slowly bring to the boil, cover and turn down to a simmer to cook for 30 minutes. Stir occasionally to stop the sauce from sticking and burning.
4 Add the remaining yoghurt, cover and cook for a further 15 minutes; by this time the sauce should be thick and the meat tender.
5 Serve sprinkled with chopped mint leaves. Accompany with steamed rice, blanched green beans and warmed roti.

COOK'S TIPS
- You can use minced lamb for an extra quick curry. Add mince after you have fried the spice paste, along with 2 cups of peeled and finely diced kumara or pumpkin to give it texture. Cook for 20 minutes. Add yoghurt and cook a further 5 minutes. Enjoy spooned onto warm naan bread with Indian condiments and warm rice.
- Rice freezes really well. If you find you have once again cooked too much, simply pack it into a plastic container or bag and freeze to have another day. It will defrost easily in the microwave, or put it into boiling water and drain to serve.
- Roti are available at most supermarkets.

The fresh flavour of apple helps cut the richness of pork. Both the fruit and apple cider are used here in what will quickly become a no-fuss favourite to serve to family and friends.

TRACEY SUNDERLAND

Drunken pork chops with parsley mash

READY IN: 35 MINUTES
SERVES: 4

Pork chops
1 Tbsp oil
4 pork loin chops
2 Tbsp butter
2 onions, peeled and sliced
2 apples, peeled and sliced
1½ cups apple cider
2 Tbsp wholegrain mustard
½ cup cream

Parsley mash
6 medium potatoes, peeled and halved
1 tsp salt
2 tsp butter
1 Tbsp chopped parsley
¼ cup milk

1 Heat a large frying pan and add the oil. Cook the pork chops for 2 minutes on each side until golden then put in a baking dish and season well with salt and pepper.
2 Add 1 Tbsp of the butter to the pan and fry the onion for 2–3 minutes until soft, then scatter over the pork.
3 Add another Tbsp butter to the pan and fry the apples until they begin to caramelise. Scatter apples over pork and onions.
4 Reheat the pan over a high heat. Pour in the apple cider, bring to the boil then allow to simmer until the liquid has reduced by half. Stir in the mustard and cream and season with salt and pepper. Bring the sauce to the boil, then pour it on top of the pork. Place in an oven preheated to 200°C and bake for 10–12 minutes.
5 Meanwhile, put the potatoes in a saucepan and cover with cold water, add salt and bring to the boil. Simmer for 12–14 minutes until soft. Drain the potatoes and leave them in the saucepan. Add butter and parsley, season with salt and pepper and mash, adding a little milk at a time, until smooth.
6 Remove pork from the oven and serve with the mash to soak up the juices and accompany with steamed vegetables.

Make the most of warm evenings with a fresh, cheerful salmon salad as a midweek dinner.

TRACEY SUNDERLAND

Hot-smoked salmon summer salad with fresh garlic mayo

READY IN: 30 MINUTES
SERVES: 4

Garlic mayo
2 egg yolks
1 tsp mild mustard
1 Tbsp white or wine vinegar
100ml canola oil
100ml olive oil
1 Tbsp lemon juice
½ clove garlic, crushed

Salad
200g gourmet potatoes, skin on
3 eggs
½ tsp salt
150g flat green beans, ends removed, cut into 4cm lengths
1 cos lettuce
1 Lebanese cucumber, partially peeled
1 green capsicum, seeds removed
6 Roma tomatoes
1 bunch radishes, cleaned, leaves removed
1 onion, finely sliced
½ cup small black olives
¼ cup parsley, chopped
200g hot-smoked salmon

1 To make the mayonnaise, place yolks into a bowl and whisk through the mustard and vinegar. Continue whisking and slowly pour in the oils until the mixture thickens and all the oil has been used. Add lemon juice and garlic and whisk through. Season to taste and add 1–2 Tbsp boiled water to thin it down slightly. (Mayonnaise can be easily and quickly made in a blender.)
2 Put clean potatoes and eggs into a saucepan, cover with water and add salt. Bring to the boil. Cook for 8 minutes. Remove eggs and place under cold running water. Leave potatoes to cook for a further 5–6 minutes. Peel eggs and cut into quarters. When the potatoes are cooked, drain and place under cold running water for a minute or so. Drain and cut into halves.
3 Blanch the beans in boiling water for 1–2 minutes and refresh in iced water. Wash the lettuce leaves, spin dry and scatter across a large flat platter.
4 Cut cucumber into thick slices, capsicum into thick wedges and tomatoes in half with the core removed. Cut the radishes into halves or, if small, leave whole.
5 Arrange salad ingredients on top of the lettuce. Top with sliced onion and black olives. Sprinkle with parsley. Break salmon into pieces and arrange on top. Serve with the mayonnaise and crusty French bread.

COOK'S TIP
• Try using fresh tuna or salmon steaks as an alternative. They are both rich types of fish so allow 80–100g per person. Sear quickly and cut into cubes to add to the salad.

Here's an exciting main-course salad idea for a quick meal. Enjoy this with a glass of chilled white wine.

TRACEY SUNDERLAND

Gruyère fritters, salad greens & sweet onion dressing

READY IN: 35 MINUTES
SERVES: 4

Salad
200g bag mixed salad leaves
   (mix of herbs, rocket, radicchio, endive)
4 leaves iceberg lettuce, washed
1 punnet cherry tomatoes

Sweet onion dressing
½ cup white wine
2 Tbsp raisins
1 large onion, finely sliced
3 Tbsp olive oil

Fritters
1½ cups soya or canola oil
250g gruyère cheese, grated
¼ cup flour
¼ tsp nutmeg
¾ tsp salt
¼ tsp white pepper
3 egg yolks
¼ cup white wine
1 Tbsp kirsch, or 1 extra Tbsp wine

1 Place salad leaves into a large bowl. Tear the iceberg lettuce into small pieces and add to the bowl. Cut half the cherry tomatoes in half and leave the remaining whole, add all to the leaves and toss through with your hands. Cover and set aside.
2 To make the dressing, pour the wine into a small bowl and cover with plastic wrap. Microwave on high for 50 seconds, then add the raisins and leave to soak.
3 Place sliced onion in a frying pan and add olive oil. Braise over a low heat until lightly cooked. This takes 2–3 minutes and the onions should be crunchy. Season to taste and stir through the wine and raisins. Remove from the heat and set aside.
4 Pour the soya or canola oil into a medium saucepan and heat while you prepare the fritters. The oil needs to be warmed slowly over a low–medium heat.
5 Place gruyère in a bowl. Sift in the flour, nutmeg, salt and pepper and stir through the cheese. Make a well in the centre and add the yolks, wine and kirsch and fold through the cheese mix.
6 Check the oil is hot enough by dropping in a tiny piece of bread. The bread needs to cook quickly and turn golden. If this happens the oil is ready, if not turn the heat up until the bread reaches this point. Use 2 dessertspoons to shape mixture into quenelles (see Glossary, page 173). Fry in batches of 3–4 fritters. Cook quickly until they turn a nice rich golden colour underneath, then turn and fry for 20–30 seconds. Remove and drain on paper towels. Keep the oil consistently hot.
7 To serve, share the salad among 4 large plates, top with 3 fritters per plate and spoon the dressing over the top.

COOK'S TIP
• Egg whites are ideal to freeze and will keep for about 2 months. Place in a small plastic container and write a date on it.

Crisp cos lettuce cups are the perfect edible vessel for holding tasty, fresh ingredients. Their beautiful spoon-shaped leaves lend themselves to being filled.

JENNIFER YEE

Tossed pork & garlic chives in cos cups

READY IN: 20 MINUTES
SERVES: 4

1 Tbsp peanut oil
½ tsp sesame oil
500g pork or chicken mince
1 long red chilli, sliced
1 small bunch garlic chives, cut into 1cm lengths
1 cup diced green beans
2 Tbsp fish sauce
1 Tbsp shaved palm sugar (see Glossary, page 173)
freshly ground black pepper, to season
small cos lettuce leaves
2 Tbsp small mint leaves
2 Tbsp deep-fried shallots (see Glossary, page 172)

1 Heat the oils in a large frying pan or wok and then add the pork or chicken mince, chilli and garlic chives. Toss to separate the mince and fry until lightly browned.
2 Add the beans and continue stir-frying for another 2 minutes before adding the fish sauce and palm sugar. Season with pepper to taste.
3 Spoon the mixture into a deep bowl to serve with a pile of crisp cos leaves. Allow about 2–3 heaped spoonfuls of filling per cos leaf. Sprinkle with fresh mint and deep-fried shallots.

COOK'S TIPS
• If you like hot chilli, choose fresh habanero or jalapeño chillies available from specialty fruit and vegetable shops.
• Almost anything goes when it comes to fillings — variations might include colourful fried rice or a warm potato salad.

Make dinner healthy and easy with a quick lamb salad that pays homage to the flavours of Greece.

TRACEY SUNDERLAND

Yoghurt-dressed roast lamb, potato & mint salad

READY IN: 25 MINUTES
SERVES: 4

Salad
4 × 125g lamb steaks, or 2 boneless lamb loins
4 Tbsp oil
12 small (400g gourmet) potatoes
1 cup Kalamata olives
150g snow peas, ends removed
130g mixed red and green oak lettuce leaves
1 red onion, finely sliced, optional
1 avocado, sliced
2 Tbsp mixed parsley and mint, finely chopped

Yoghurt dressing
½ cup thick natural yoghurt
2 Tbsp mint, finely sliced
½ clove garlic, crushed

To serve
2 Tbsp mint sauce

1 Season lamb with salt and freshly ground pepper. Heat a frying pan to medium-hot and add 2 Tbsp oil. Sear the lamb on each side for 1 minute. Remove and place on an oven tray, then return pan to the heat.
2 Cut the potatoes into quarters lengthways. Add to the pan with extra oil and brown for 5 minutes. Remove and place on the oven tray. Add olives. Roast in oven preheated to 180°C for 8 minutes.
3 Remove the lamb and place on a plate to rest. Roast the potatoes and olives for a further 3-5 minutes or until the potatoes have turned golden.
4 Blanch snow peas in boiling water for 30 seconds then refresh in iced water then dry with kitchen paper. The snow peas should be crisp.
5 In a large bowl toss together the lettuce leaves, red onion, avocado and parsley and mint mix. Add the blanched snow peas.
6 Mix together the yoghurt, mint and garlic.
7 Cut lamb into large cubes. Add to salad bowl with potatoes and olives. Drizzle mint sauce over. Pour yoghurt and mint dressing on top. Toss lightly. Or serve the salad as separate components with the yoghurt on the side and the mint sauce drizzled over.

COOK'S TIPS
• For a quick and easy dressing you could buy a cucumber, yoghurt and mint dip and stir some fresh mint and basil through it. Use any leftover dressing as a dip the next day.
• Try using kumara in place of the potato. Cut it into thick slices and then in half again before pan-frying. Roast kumara for the same length of time as the potatoes and, because kumara cooks a little quicker, it will caramelise and be a little crispy.

This quick fish dinner uses four key ingredients: fish, potatoes, lemon and parsley. Nothing could be simpler.

TRACEY SUNDERLAND

Fish pie with spring onion mash

READY IN: 1 HOUR
SERVES: 4–6

4 large potatoes (750g), peeled
6 medium-textured fish fillets (750g), such as blue cod, gurnard or snapper
2½ cups milk
1 clove garlic, squashed
5 Tbsp butter
1 onion, sliced
3 Tbsp flour
½ cup cheese, grated
½ tsp smoked paprika
4 spring onions, finely sliced
2 Tbsp parsley, chopped
juice of 1 lemon
2 Tbsp sour cream

1 Dice the potatoes and simmer for approximately 12 minutes or until tender. Drain, put back into the saucepan and put aside.
2 Place whole fish fillets, milk and garlic in a saucepan and simmer for 2 minutes. Remove from heat and stand for 3 minutes. Remove fish with a slotted spoon and place in a greased baking dish, breaking fish into large pieces to cover the base. Strain, and keep, the cooking liquid.
3 Melt 2 Tbsp butter in a saucepan, add onion and cook on low heat for 5 minutes, or until golden. Sprinkle in the flour, stir with a wooden spoon and cook for 2 minutes. Continue stirring and slowly add the cooking liquid. Bring to the boil, reduce heat to low and cook until sauce thickens. Add cheese and paprika, season and stir well. Pour sauce over fish.
4 Mash cooked potatoes with 3 Tbsp butter, stir in spring onions, parsley, lemon juice and sour cream, season to taste with salt and pepper. Place large spoons of mash on top of the fish, place in oven at 200°C for 10–15 minutes until the potato is golden.

COOK'S TIP
- Always check for bones before cooking by running fingers carefully over the fish.
- Buy a pair of eyebrow tweezers exclusively for removing bones from fish without cutting away the fillet. Sterilise the tweezers after each use.

This is a sure-to-please midweek meal idea that's best served with new season potatoes.

TRACEY SUNDERLAND

Pan-fried fish with lemon, caper & parsley sauce

READY IN: 35 MINUTES
SERVES: 4

Fish
8 small medium-textured fish fillets, without skin (see Cook's Tip)
4 Tbsp flour

Lemon, caper & parsley sauce
½ cup white wine
juice of 1 lemon
parsley stalks
¼ tsp whole peppercorns
2 Tbsp capers, finely chopped
¼ cup chopped parsley
100g cold butter, cubed
2 Tbsp butter, to fry
2 Tbsp oil, to fry
new potatoes and seasonal green vegetables, to serve

1 Run your fingers over the fish fillets to remove any scales. Place flour in a dish and dust each fillet well. Set aside.
2 In a small saucepan place wine, lemon juice, parsley stalks and peppercorns. Bring to the boil and simmer gently until reduced by two thirds. Strain to remove stalks and peppercorns. There should be about ¼ cup liquid remaining; pour it back into the pot and place the pot on the element.
3 Stir in capers and parsley, then remove from the heat. Add butter, cube by cube, and stir until dissolved and the sauce looks lightly thickened. Place saucepan in a warm place while you cook the fish.
4 Heat butter and oil in a frying pan over medium heat. Add fish fillets and cook for approximately 1 minute on each side.
5 Serve fish with the caper and parsley sauce spooned over. Accompany with new potatoes and seasonal greens.

COOK'S TIP
• Cook fresh fish simply, with a few flavours that enhance rather than overpower. Pan-frying is ideal. Choose medium-textured fillets, such as blue cod, gurnard, John dory, snapper, terakihi and warehou.

If you are strapped for time and need an easy meal that still tastes great, this recipe is it.
LAURIE BLACK

Mushrooms on toast with soft onion, sherry & capers

READY IN: 20 MINUTES
SERVES: 2

2 Tbsp olive oil
1 medium onion, thinly sliced
1 clove garlic, sliced
1 sprig rosemary
1 tsp salt
25g butter
5 large flat-cap mushrooms, brushed clean, stems trimmed, cut in half
1 tsp thyme leaves or chopped parsley
½ cup medium or Amontillado sherry
1 tsp capers
4 slices ciabatta or crusty bread
green salad, to serve

1 Heat 1 Tbsp olive oil in a pan over a low heat and add onion, garlic, rosemary and ½ tsp salt. Stir, cover and cook for 5 minutes or until the onion is soft, but not browning. Discard the rosemary sprig.
2 Meanwhile, heat another 1 Tbsp oil in a frying pan over a medium-high heat. Add butter and, once sizzling, add mushrooms and thyme. Brown mushrooms on each side then sprinkle with ½ tsp salt.
3 Add sherry to the pan and allow to simmer for 4 minutes. Add capers and remove the pan from the heat.
4 Grill bread on a hot, ridged grill pan, or chargrill. Place on warm plates. Pile some onion onto each slice. Serve mushrooms on top. Season with freshly ground black pepper and serve with a green salad.

This delicious tart is a dinner option your family will love. It's also ideal to pack for a picnic.

TRACEY SUNDERLAND

Chicken, spinach & mushroom tart

READY IN: 1 HOUR
SERVES: 4

2 squares pre-rolled short pastry
2 Tbsp oil
2 onions, sliced
2 cups button mushrooms, sliced
130g packet washed spinach leaves
4 eggs
¼ tsp salt
pinch of nutmeg
300ml cream
1 cup grated gruyère cheese
1 cooked chicken breast, finely sliced

1 Grease a 27cm × 19cm tart tin well and press one pastry square into the tin to line the sides and base. One sheet will not cover the whole tin completely. Cut ¼ of the second sheet and use to finish lining the tin. Use your fingers to press the seams of the two pastry sheets together. Make sure pastry is pressed in well and there are no air bubbles. Place tin in fridge and leave to chill. Keep remaining pastry for another recipe.
2 Heat oil in a hot pan and sauté the onions until soft. Remove from the pan and leave to cool. Add mushrooms to the pan and stir until they begin to wilt, remove and drain free of water. Add spinach to pan with a splash of water, cover and cook until wilted. Remove from pan, place in sieve and run under cold water to stop it cooking. Drain and put aside.
3 Mix eggs with salt, nutmeg and freshly ground black pepper to taste, then whisk in cream.
4 Remove tart tin from fridge and scatter onion over the chilled pastry. Lay grated cheese on top of the onion, then add mushrooms, spinach and chicken. Pour egg filling over the top. Place in the middle of an oven preheated to 220°C. Cook for 40–45 minutes until tart rises in the centre.
5 Serve the tart with a rocket or green salad on the side.

Using chicken, mushrooms, eggs and onions, this is a satisfying family meal for all seasons.

TRACEY SUNDERLAND

Parmesan crumbed chicken scaloppine with polenta

READY IN: 35 MINUTES
SERVES: 4

Chicken
4 single skinless chicken breasts
2 eggs
¼ tsp salt
2½ cups fresh breadcrumbs
½ cup grated parmesan
½ cup flour

Polenta
4 cups water
1 tsp salt
1 cup instant polenta
½ cup grated parmesan

To serve
3 Tbsp oil
2 red onions, finely sliced
2 cups button mushrooms, sliced

1 Cut breasts in half horizontally. Place plastic wrap on chopping board, put one chicken piece on top, cover with wrap. Beat to even thickness with a meat mallet or rolling pin. Repeat until you have 8 even-sized scaloppine (see Glossary, page 173).
2 Beat eggs and salt together. Mix breadcrumbs and parmesan on a separate plate. Dust each scaloppine with flour, dip into egg and coat with bread and cheese mix.
3 Bring salted water to the boil. Gradually add polenta, stirring constantly. Once added, stir for 5 minutes until mixture thickens. Add parmesan and season with freshly ground black pepper.
4 Heat enough oil to coat the base of a frying pan and sauté the chicken for 1–2 minutes on each side. Do in 2 batches, placing in a low oven to keep warm.
5 In the pan, fry onion until soft, add mushrooms. Cook until liquid evaporates and onion begins to brown. Place a large spoonful of polenta on each plate, top with chicken and sprinkle with onion mix.

COOK'S TIPS
• To make 100g fresh breadcrumbs use 4 slices of white toast bread, remove crusts and pulse in a blender or food processor until small crumbs form.
• Freeze breadcrumbs to use in recipes such as this one, as a topping or to add to meatballs and burger patties. They don't need to be defrosted — simply sprinkle over or stir through a dish.

Here's a handy midweek meal idea using mussels. Simply serve with a wedge of lemon and a salad.

TRACEY SUNDERLAND

Wood-smoked mussel & zucchini fritters

READY IN: 30 MINUTES
MAKES: 8 FRITTERS

375g pottle marinated wood-smoked mussels
2 medium zucchini, grated
1 red onion, finely diced
2 Tbsp parsley, chopped
2 eggs
1 cup flour
1 tsp baking powder
1 tsp salt
½ tsp ground white pepper
½ cup milk
3 Tbsp butter, melted
oil, to fry

To serve
sliced avocado
lemon wedges
salad greens

1 Drain mussels and chop finely with a sharp knife. Place in a bowl, add zucchini, red onion, parsley and eggs and mix well with a fork.
2 Sift flour, baking powder, salt and pepper into a large bowl. Make a well in the centre, add the mussel and vegetable mixture, pour the milk over and stir to combine. Add the butter and whisk lightly through the fritter mix.
3 Preheat a non-stick frying pan or barbecue plate. Drizzle over a little oil and heat to medium. Cook 2–3 fritters at a time, using 2 Tbsp of the mix for each one. Adjust the heat as needed. Cook the fritters for 2–3 minutes until small bubbles form all over the surface then turn over and cook for another 1–2 minutes, until crispy. Layer with sliced avocado and serve with a wedge of lemon and a salad.

COOK'S TIPS
- If wood-smoked mussels are not available, use plain marinated mussels instead.
- If you have only ordinary flour, and no baking powder, use beer in place of milk. It's a great raising agent and also helps to make the fritters light and crispy.

Cannelloni doesn't have to be fiddly to make — use sheets of fresh pasta cut to size and rolled up to encase the filling.

TRACEY SUNDERLAND

Field mushroom cannelloni

READY IN: 1 HOUR
SERVES: 6

Filling
250g flat portobello mushrooms
2 large onions, sliced
6 tomatoes, cut into quarters
2 Tbsp oil

Béchamel sauce
2 Tbsp butter
3 Tbsp flour
1½ cups milk
250g crème fraîche
½ cup grated tasty cheese

Cannelloni
400g packet fresh plain lasagne sheets
1½ cup basil leaves
½ cup grated parmesan
2 Tbsp chopped marjoram, chervil or parsley, to serve

1 Preheat the oven to 200°C. To make the filling, brush dirt from the mushrooms with a paper towel or small brush then slice thickly. Place in a shallow oven tray with onion and tomato quarters. Season well with salt and pepper and drizzle with oil. Place in the oven and cook for 20 minutes until soft then remove the tray from the oven. Turn oven down to 180°C.
2 Meanwhile, make béchamel sauce by melting the butter in a saucepan over a low heat. Stir in the flour and let the mixture bubble for a minute. Slowly add the milk, half a cup at a time, stirring constantly until the sauce thickens. Add the crème fraîche and tasty cheese. Turn up the heat and bring back to the boil. The sauce needs to be smooth and it should only just coat the back of a spoon. Season to taste with salt and pepper. Remove from the heat and set aside.
3 Lay six lasagne sheets out on a board one on top of the other, and cut the pile in half to make 12 rectangles, each approximately 7cm x 13cm.
4 To make the cannelloni, take a pasta rectangle and lay a little onion, mushroom and 2 quarters of roast tomato in the centre. Add a few basil leaves and roll into a tube by turning the longer side over and then place the seam-side down in a greased, large shallow baking dish. Repeat, laying each cannelloni beside the other.
5 At this stage the béchamel sauce should still be warm and quite thin so it will pour easily over the cannelloni and soak through the raw pasta, helping it to cook nicely. Scatter parmesan over the cannelloni, put the dish in the preheated oven and cook for 20-25 minutes. Sprinkle with herbs and serve with a crisp salad.

This hearty meal idea is certainly on my list of favourites, and you'll be lucky if there are any leftovers.

TRACEY SUNDERLAND

Prosciutto chicken wraps with chunky oven chips

READY IN: 30 MINUTES
SERVES: 4

6 large potatoes, skin on, scrubbed
3 Tbsp oil
75g prosciutto, sliced
400g chicken tenderloin fillets
fresh sage leaves

1 Cut the potatoes into large even chunks and put them on an oven tray. Drizzle with 2 Tbsp of oil and season generously with salt and pepper. Toss to coat well. Place in an oven preheated to 200°C. (They will need 25–30 minutes total cooking time.)
2 Lay prosciutto slices out on a board. With a sharp knife cut each slice into thirds lengthways.
3 Place chicken fillets on a large plate and season with salt and pepper. Place a couple of sage leaves lengthways on each fillet, then wrap a piece of prosciutto tightly around to cover the length of each fillet. Repeat until finished and place the fillets back on the plate.
4 Preheat a frying pan, add the remaining oil and sear the fillets quickly on each side until lightly golden (about 2 minutes). Place them in the oven directly on top of the chips (which should be nearly ready and crisping up nicely) and cook for a further 6 minutes. Serve with salad or spring vegetables.

COOK'S TIPS
- Prosciutto is a cured bacon product available in the deli section of your supermarket with sliced bacon and ham.
- If you cannot find prosciutto you could try using streaky bacon instead. Bacon is cut thicker than prosciutto so you may need to secure it to the chicken fillets with a toothpick and cook for a little longer in the frying pan.

Scrub up the barbecue and whip up these smashing burgers for a satisfying outdoor dinner.

TRACEY SUNDERLAND

Lamb burgers with roast peppers & fried onion

READY IN: 35 MINUTES
SERVES: 4

Patties
- 500g minced lamb
- 100g fresh breadcrumbs (see Cook's Tip, page 58)
- ¼ cup fresh herbs, chopped (such as mint, parsley and rosemary)
- 1 tsp salt
- ½ tsp ground pepper
- 1 egg
- 2 Tbsp flour, to shape patties

Filling
- 1 red pepper
- 2 Tbsp olive oil
- 2 small onions, skins removed
- ¼ cup thick mayonnaise
- 1 buttercrunch lettuce, washed
- 1 avocado, sliced
- ¼ cup tomato relish
- 1 loaf ciabatta or Turkish bread

1 To make meat patties, place lamb mince, breadcrumbs, chopped herbs, salt and pepper into a bowl. Mix well with a fork. Make a well in the centre and break in the egg. Mix until combined.
2 With your hands, shape the mix into 4 even-sized balls. Using a little flour, press each into an oval shape of even thickness. Place on a lightly floured plate and chill while you prepare the other ingredients (about 10 minutes).
3 Cut the pepper into quarters and remove stalk and seeds. Put on a plate and toss in a little oil. Cut the onions into large, thick rings and place on the plate with the peppers.
4 Add a little oil to the preheated hotplate of the barbecue and cook lamb patties and onion rings on an even low-to-medium heat. The patties should take about 6 minutes each side. Cook the peppers over the grill at the same time, turning as required. When cooked, move the onions and peppers to a cooler part of the barbecue. Remove the patties to a plate and rest for a few minutes.
5 Cut the loaf of bread lengthways through the middle, then into 4 even pieces to make into burger buns. Grill the bread pieces on each side for a couple of minutes until warm and slightly golden.
6 To compile the lamb burgers, line up the bases on a board and spread with a little mayonnaise, add 2 lettuce leaves, cut each ¼ of pepper in half and place on lettuce, then add a lamb patty and the avocado slices. Spread burger tops with tomato relish and press on top to finish. Serve with grilled onion rings.

COOK'S TIP
- These minced lamb patties will freeze easily — just place each patty between waxed paper sheets and pop into a freezer bag.

Simple and succulent, this fresh take on grilled chicken is a sure-fire winner.

TRACEY SUNDERLAND

Chicken steaks with green olive salsa

READY IN: 20 MINUTES
SERVES: 4

Marinade
- 1 clove garlic, crushed
- ½ tsp honey, warmed
- 2 Tbsp lemon juice
- ¼ cup olive oil
- ¼ cup fresh oregano, chopped

- 2 × 300g skinless chicken breasts

Salsa
- 1 cup green stuffed olives, finely sliced
- 1 green pepper, seeds removed, finely diced
- 4 spring onions, finely sliced
- ½ red onion, finely diced
- 2 Tbsp olive oil
- 2 Tbsp white wine vinegar

1 In a small bowl whisk together the garlic, honey, lemon juice, olive oil and oregano.
2 Slice each chicken breast in half horizontally and lengthways to make 4 even-sized steaks. Season the chicken to taste with salt and pepper, put into a shallow dish and pour the marinade over. Turn steaks and coat well in marinade, then put aside (see Cook's Tip).
3 For the salsa, combine olives, green pepper, spring onions and red onion. Pour in olive oil and vinegar, and season to taste with salt and freshly ground black pepper. Toss salsa with a spoon to coat all ingredients with oil and vinegar. Transfer to a serving bowl.
4 Preheat barbecue grill-plate to medium. Place chicken on grill and add a little marinade, instead of oil, to cook it. Sear chicken for approximately 3½ minutes on each side until cooked through.
5 Top each chicken steak with olive salsa and serve with a crispy salad, fresh vegetables (we used snow beans, see Glossary, page 173) and baked potatoes.

COOK'S TIP
- Always leave marinating meat in the bottom of the fridge and, to avoid contaminating other foods, cover with plastic wrap or, even better, place in a container with a lid. Shake now and then to cover the chicken well in marinade.

Try making this with different tube-shaped pasta, such as penne, rigatoni or trenne, to make it more interesting. The tubular shapes will hold the sauce and moisture.

TRACEY SUNDERLAND

Four-cheese baked macaroni

READY IN: 40 MINUTES
SERVES: 6

2 Tbsp oil
1 onion, peeled and roughly sliced
2 cups macaroni
250g tub cottage cheese
1 cup grated gruyère cheese
½ cup crumbled blue vein cheese
½ cup milk
½ cup fresh breadcrumbs (see Cook's Tip, page 58)
½ cup grated parmesan
2 rashers bacon, finely diced, optional
1 Tbsp chopped chives

1 Preheat the oven to 200°C. Heat a frying pan and add the oil. Toss in the sliced onion and cook for 5 minutes until soft and lightly golden then put aside.
2 Meanwhile, cook the macaroni until al dente, about 6–8 minutes. Drain in a colander and put back into the saucepan. Add the cooked onion, cottage cheese, gruyère and blue vein cheeses. Pour the milk over and season well with salt and pepper. Stir though then tip into a medium-sized, greased baking dish.
3 Sprinkle with breadcrumbs and parmesan and top with finely diced bacon, if using, and place in the oven to cook for 25–30 minutes.
4 Sprinkle with chives and serve immediately.

COOK'S TIP
• For a more child-friendly version of this dish, you may wish to omit the blue cheese from the recipe — you can crumble the blue cheese over the top and reheat the macaroni later on for the adults.

Mussels are available all year round and are a good source of iron. Try this easy all-in-one meal when you want to impress friends — let everyone help themselves.

TRACEY SUNDERLAND

Green lip mussels, fresh herbs & pasta

READY IN: 35 MINUTES
SERVES: 4

- 2 cups firmly packed herbs - a mix of at least 3 of parsley, basil, coriander and mint
- 2 cloves garlic
- 4 smoked oysters or 3 anchovy fillets
- 2 tsp capers
- ¼ cup lemon juice
- ¼ cup olive oil
- 2 tsp salt
- 500g conchiglie pasta (small shells)
- 1kg fresh small mussels in shells, cleaned (see Cook's Tip)
- ½ cup wine
- ½ cup water
- ½ onion, finely diced
- ½ cup chopped flat leaf parsley
- 1 cup shaved parmesan

1 Place the mix of herbs, garlic, smoked oysters or anchovies, capers and lemon juice into a food processor. Pulse until finely chopped then slowly pour in the oil. The sauce should be a rich green colour and quite thick. Set aside.
2 Bring a large saucepan of water to the boil and add salt. When the water is rolling, add dried pasta shells and cook for 6–8 minutes, or until al dente.
3 Meanwhile, place cleaned mussels, wine, water and onion into a saucepan, cover with a lid and place on a high heat. Steam the mussels for 2 minutes then check to see they are open. If not, cover and cook for a further 30 seconds (don't overcook, as they will be tough). Remove and discard any mussels that have not opened. Check all the beards have been removed from the mussels.
4 Drain the cooked pasta in a colander then add pasta to the mussel pot. Stir in half the green sauce and toss quickly. Serve in a large, deep pasta-serving bowl and drizzle with remaining green sauce. Scatter with parsley and parmesan and season with freshly ground black pepper.

COOK'S TIP

- To clean mussels, remove the tough hairy beard from the mussel. Hold the mussel in one hand and tug sharply upwards on the hair coming from the shell. It should release if you are quick. Put the mussels in a clean sink and scrub. Rinse. The shells should be smooth and free of debris.

Take the chill off cool evenings with this filling Mexican meal.

TRACEY SUNDERLAND

Chicken & chilli enchiladas

READY IN: 30–35 MINUTES
SERVES: 4–5

4 Tbsp oil
1 red onion, finely diced
1 red chilli, seeds removed, finely sliced
350g chicken mince
½x425g can chilli beans
280g packet enchilada tortillas
375g jar enchilada simmer sauce
1 cup feta, crumbled
1 cup colby cheese, grated
3 Tbsp finely chopped parsley or coriander, to serve

1 Heat a frying pan to a medium heat and add 2 Tbsp oil. Add onion and chilli and sauté for 2–3 minutes until soft. Remove from the pan to a plate and return the pan to the heat.
2 Turn the pan up to high and add remaining oil. Add the chicken mince and pan-fry until lightly golden, breaking it up as you go with a wooden spoon. This will take about 3 minutes.
3 Stir in the chilli beans, return the sautéed onion and chilli and simmer for 2 minutes. Remove from the heat and season to taste, adding extra chilli if preferred.
4 To make the enchiladas, warm the tortillas first, according to the instructions on the packet. This enables the tortillas to be separated without tearing. Place a tortilla on a board, spoon 2 Tbsp filling into the centre then wrap and place seam-side down in a greased, shallow ovenproof dish. Repeat until you have 10 tortillas.
5 Cover the enchiladas generously with the sauce. Sprinkle with feta and grated cheese and bake in the oven at 180°C for 10–12 minutes.
6 Just as you serve, sprinkle with chopped parsley or coriander. Enjoy with a crunchy salad and sour cream on the side.

COOK'S TIP
• Chilli plants are very easy to grow at home. Plant them in the hottest part of the garden, then all they require is lots of water.

Spice up midweek meals with a hot bowl of chilli. Serve on rice with a dollop of sour cream and avocado salsa on top.

TRACEY SUNDERLAND

Beef & bean chilli with avocado salsa

READY IN: 1 HOUR 5 MINUTES
SERVES: 6

Chilli
4 Tbsp oil
1 red onion, finely diced
1 jalapeño chilli, seeds removed, finely sliced
2 cloves garlic, crushed
1 bunch coriander, washed
800g beef chuck steak
400g can Mexican tomatoes
½ cup tomato purée
1 cup beef stock
1 red pepper, seeds and stalk removed
300g can red kidney beans, drained
juice of 1 lime
½ cup sour cream, to serve

Avocado salsa
1 avocado, diced
1 tomato, diced
2 Tbsp chopped coriander leaves
juice of 1 lime

1 Heat a heavy-based saucepan to a medium heat and add 2 Tbsp oil. Add onion, chilli and garlic and sauté for 1 minute. Trim off and discard the stringy roots from the coriander. Slice the coriander stalks finely until about half way up. Put the bunch of coriander leaves aside to use later in this recipe and add all the stalks to the saucepan. Continue to sauté over a low heat for 2–3 minutes. When soft remove the ingredients from the pan and put aside.
2 Trim away any fat from the chuck steak. Cut the steak into small dice, approximately 1cm. Heat a saucepan to high and add 1 Tbsp oil. Fry half the beef until well browned, 2–3 minutes, then remove and add to the onion. Brown the second batch of beef, then leave it in the pan.
3 Add the sautéed onion and beef to the saucepan then stir in the Mexican tomatoes, purée and beef stock. Stir and bring to the boil, stir again and turn down to a simmer. Cover and cook for 30 minutes. Ensure you stir regularly to ensure the contents do not burn.
4 Meanwhile, cut red pepper into wide wedges, and then into large squares. Roughly chop the coriander leaves and reserve 2 Tbsp for the salsa.
5 When the beef chilli has cooked for 30 minutes, add the red pepper and kidney beans. Stir, then cover and simmer for a further 20 minutes or until meat is tender.
6 To make the salsa, put the avocado, tomato, coriander and lime juice in a bowl. Season generously with salt and pepper. Turn the ingredients gently with a spoon once or twice.
7 Stir the reserved, chopped coriander leaves and lime juice into the beef chilli and season to taste. Serve on rice with a dollop of sour cream and the refreshing avocado salsa on top.

Taste
entertaining

The intense tangy flavour of dried blueberries is a great match for pork, but you could use cranberries or currants instead.

ALLYSON GOFTON

Roast pork with dried blueberry & nut stuffing

READY IN: 2 HOURS
SERVES: 8

1 cup fresh white breadcrumbs (see Cook's Tip, page 58)
½ cup dried blueberries
½ cup sliced toasted almonds or sliced toasted macadamia nuts
½ tsp ground allspice
2–3 Tbsp chopped fresh sage leaves
75g butter, melted
2.5kg boned loin of pork with a long flap, well scored
lemon juice, optional

1 Toss together the breadcrumbs, dried blueberries, nuts, allspice, sage and butter. Season with salt and pepper.
2 Place the pork, skin-side down, on a chopping board and press on the stuffing firmly, close to the meaty fillet. Roll up to enclose the stuffing and secure the pork roll with string or skewers. Rub the pork skin well with salt and lemon juice or salt and oil. This will help the skin to crackle.
3 Roast in a hot (220°C) oven for 15 minutes and then lower the temperature to 170°C and cook for a further 1–1¼ hours. The crackling should be crisp and the meat cooked. When pierced with a meat fork the juice should run clear. If pink, continue cooking. Pork is cooked when its internal temperature is 71°C (measure with a cooking thermometer).
4 Remove from the oven and allow to rest for 10 minutes before carving and serving with your favourite accompaniments.

COOK'S TIP
- Dried blueberries can be found in specialty food shops.

A well-rested roasted Scotch fillet of beef melts in the mouth. You need very little to accompany such a delicious prime cut.

ALLYSON GOFTON

Sage & peppered scotch fillet with fresh cream sauce

READY IN: 2 HOURS
SERVES: 8

Beef
2 Tbsp dried green peppercorns, coarsely crushed
2kg piece Scotch fillet of beef
4-6 large stems rosemary
6-8 sprigs sage
flaky salt, for seasoning

Sauce
2 cups cream
grated rind and juice of 1 lemon (not Meyer)
1½ Tbsp prepared smooth French mustard
2 Tbsp wholeseed mustard
¼ cup chopped or minced chives
1 tsp salt
2 tsp horseradish sauce, optional

1 Crush the peppercorns by placing them on a chopping board and pressing the edge of a heavy-based saucepan on top. (They will be coarsely crushed.)
2 Rub the crushed peppercorns into the beef. Arrange the herbs on top and secure with string. Season with salt.
3 Place the beef on a foil-lined tray, cover and allow to rest at room temperature for about 30 minutes.
4 To make the sauce, whip the cream, lemon rind and juice together until soft peaks form. Stir in the mustards, chives, salt and horseradish, if using.
5 Roast the fillet at 190°C for 80 minutes for medium-rare meat. Remove from the oven and let stand 10 minutes before carving. If wished, remove the cooked, dried herbs and add some fresh ones for presentation. Serve with the cream mustard sauce.

COOK'S TIPS
• If the fillet is more or less than 2kg, allow 20 minutes per 500g for medium-rare meat. For well-done meat, roast the fillet for 25 minutes per 500g.
• The beef can be prepared the day before and kept wrapped or covered in the refrigerator overnight. Remove from the refrigerator, keep covered and stand at room temperature for 1 hour before cooking.

Serve friends this beautifully presented and filling feast of salmon for a special dinner.

ALLYSON GOFTON

Lemon & pepper salmon with béarnaise sauce

READY IN: 1 HOUR
SERVES: 6

Salmon
6 × 200g salmon fillets
2 Tbsp white peppercorns, crushed
¼ cup lemon-scented olive oil (or use plain)
grated rind 1 lemon
1 tsp crushed flaky salt
fresh herbs, to garnish

To serve
600g asparagus

Béarnaise sauce
½ shallot, peeled and finely diced
2–3 peppercorns
2 Tbsp white wine or tarragon vinegar
2 Tbsp water
125g unsalted butter
2 egg yolks
1 Tbsp each chopped tarragon and chervil
lemon juice

1 Cut each fillet in half and place into a shallow container. Sprinkle with the peppercorns, lemon-scented olive oil, lemon rind and flaky salt. Cover and set aside for about 20 minutes.
2 For the sauce, put the diced shallot, peppercorns, wine or vinegar and water in a saucepan and simmer over a low heat until reduced to 2 Tbsp of liquid. Drain and keep.
3 Melt the butter and keep warm. Mix the egg yolks with the strained, reduced vinegar mix in a double saucepan or heat-proof bowl. Place over a saucepan of simmering water and gradually whisk in the melted butter to make a thick sauce. Stir in the chopped herbs. Season with salt and freshly ground black pepper and a squeeze of lemon juice.
4 Trim the ends of the asparagus and peel the stems from about half way down. Place into boiling water and bring back to the boil and cook for 1 minute. Remove from the heat and place into a hot frying pan with a little oil or butter and cook until lightly browned. Alternatively, this can be done on a barbecue. The asparagus can also be blanched and refreshed in cold water ahead of time and then grilled just before serving.
5 Heat a frying pan until very hot and place the salmon pieces in, flesh-side down. (Always place fish in a pan the side down you wish to serve uppermost to your guests.) Cook for 2 minutes and then turn. Cook a further 2–3 minutes or until the salmon is medium. It should flake but not be overcooked (see Cook's Tip). Remove from the pan and place quickly onto a plate. Spoon over the béarnaise sauce and arrange grilled asparagus on top. Garnish with herbs such as chervil, chives, parsley and tarragon, or a mixture of these.

COOK'S TIP
• I like salmon to be cooked so that the fillet flakes easily but remains moist. You can tell by looking at the side of the salmon fillets while they cook: the flesh will turn a dull pink colour. Remove it from the pan just as this happens.

Create a flavourful and authentic Asian meal using aromatic spices. This seafood dish uses Szechwan pepper, a toasty and peppery spice.

JENNIFER YEE

Salt & pepper chilli prawns & squid

READY IN: 45 MINUTES
SERVES: 4

Batter
1 cup cornflour
2 eggs
2/3 cup cold water
pinch salt

Seafood
1 litre vegetable oil
16 baby squid tubes, opened and scored (see Cook's Tip)
3 dozen green prawns, shelled, deveined, tails left on
4 spring onions, sliced diagonally
4 cloves garlic, chopped finely
3 dried chillies, crushed or 2 small red chillies, sliced
1 Tbsp salt
1 Tbsp toasted Szechwan peppercorns, crushed in mortar and pestle
lime wedges, optional

1 Make batter by mixing cornflour, egg, water and salt together until smooth. The batter should be very runny.
2 Heat the vegetable oil in a wok or saucepan until a cube of bread sizzles when dropped in. Coat squid pieces and prawns with batter and drop into hot oil. Cook squid until it curls up and the batter is crisp. Fry prawns for about 4 minutes until golden. Remove with a slotted spoon and leave to drain on kitchen paper, keeping warm.
3 Pour most of the oil out of the wok, leaving only 1–2 Tbsp. Reheat, add spring onions, garlic and chillies. Quickly stir-fry for 2 minutes and then return prawns and squid to the wok. Toss everything together quickly before sprinkling with salt and crushed peppercorns. Make sure everything is well mixed. Serve piping hot with lime wedges, if desired.

COOK'S TIP
• Cut baby squid along their natural groove and open flat. Wipe dry with a paper towel and score in a criss-cross pattern.

This is an updated version of my mother's traditional roast lamb — perfect for a large gathering.

LAURIE BLACK

Perfect roast lamb

READY IN: 2 HOURS 10 MINUTES
SERVES: 6

- 2kg carvery roast
- 2 cloves garlic, thickly sliced
- 2 × 10cm sprigs rosemary
- 1 Tbsp light olive oil
- 1 tsp salt
- 1 cup white wine
- 2 cups water
- ½ cup good-quality reduced beef stock, optional

1 Using a small sharp knife, cut 8–12 evenly spaced slits into the meaty parts of the lamb leg. Tuck a slice of garlic into each slit.
2 Gently pluck 8–12 little bunches of rosemary leaves from the base of the sprigs and tuck each one beside a slice of garlic. Rub oil all over the outside of the lamb. Sprinkle with the salt and rub this in too.
3 Wrap cotton string a couple of times around the meaty end of the leg to hold it in shape. Place the lamb in a roasting pan on top of the remaining rosemary. Add wine and water.
4 Roast the lamb at 210°C for 1 hour for just-pink meat (or 13–15 minutes for every 0.5kg). Remove cooked lamb to a large plate, cover loosely with foil. Set aside near the oven to rest for 15 minutes before carving. Meanwhile, pour pan juices into a jug, skim the fat from the surface (or use a special fat-separating jug) and discard with rosemary sprigs. Return juices to pan and taste. If watery, boil to reduce slightly. Add beef stock (if using), bring to gentle boil for 2 minutes, then remove from heat.
5 Remove string from the meat and, starting at the widest end, cut thin slices of lamb. Serve on warmed plates and spoon over some pan juices. Put remaining juices into a warmed gravy boat. Serve with roast potatoes and steamed greens or a simple salad.

Tzatziki is a refreshing yoghurt sauce, made variously with cucumber, mint, garlic and lemon. This is a very simple version.

LAURIE BLACK

Fish wrapped in vine leaves with tzatziki

READY IN: 12 MINUTES
SERVES: 6

Tzatziki
½ small telegraph cucumber, halved lengthwise
150ml yoghurt
iodised sea salt

Fish
3 bottled vine leaves (from supermarkets and delis),
   rinsed, patted dry and brushed with olive oil
6 small or 3 large pieces fresh white fish fillets (600g),
   skin left on, cut apart if joined at the top (see Cook's Tips)
olive oil, for cooking
lemon wedges, for serving

1 Using a spoon, scrape all the seeds out of the cucumber and discard them. Cut the cucumber into 1cm dice. Combine with yoghurt and season with a pinch of salt. Tzatziki can be refrigerated for a couple of hours if necessary.
2 If the fish fillets are small, cut each vine leaf in half. Place a vine leaf, rib-side down, on a clean work surface. Place fish fillet on top, skin-side up and wrap the edges of the leaf firmly around to the skin side of the fish. Transfer to a plate until ready to cook. If fish fillets are large, wrap each in a whole vine leaf, in the manner above, and use a sharp knife to cut the leaf-wrapped pieces in half. Rub a little salt onto the exposed areas of fish skin.
3 Heat a little olive oil to medium hot in a large frying pan. Carefully place fish, skin-side down, into the pan. Fry for 2 minutes then carefully turn each piece over. Cook briefly until fish is white all the way through.
4 Spoon some tzatziki onto each plate and place a piece of fried fish on top. Serve with lemon wedges.

COOK'S TIPS
- Always choose the freshest fish fillets you can find.
- Use small fillets of fish whole or slice up larger ones once they've been wrapped in a vine leaf.

Combined with the flavours of the Mediterranean, lamb makes a refreshing change for a dinner party.

LAURIE BLACK

Herb-scented barbecued lamb with olive paste & skordalia

READY IN: 1 HOUR
SERVES: 6

Lamb
6 small lamb fillets, trimmed of any silverskin
good-quality olive oil, to coat lamb
2 Tbsp fresh oregano leaves
leaves from 2 sprigs thyme
black pepper, coarsely ground

Skordalia
2 whole bulbs garlic
1 Tbsp water
1 tsp oil
4 medium-large floury potatoes, such as Agria, peeled and cut in large chunks
½ cup olive oil, warmed

To serve
⅓ cup black olive paste (see Glossary, page 172)
1 Tbsp extra virgin olive oil
green beans, to serve

1 Place lamb fillets in a container and coat with a dash of olive oil. Add the oregano and thyme leaves and plenty of black pepper. Cover and refrigerate for at least 30 minutes or up to 12 hours.
2 Meanwhile, rub loose bits off the garlic, then wrap in foil, adding 1 Tbsp of water and 1 tsp oil to the parcel. Bake at 200°C for about 30 minutes until garlic is tender. Cut the base off each bulb and squeeze the garlic out using the back of a cook's knife. Discard the papery husks.
3 Steam or boil the potatoes until very tender. Add the garlic flesh to the drained potatoes and mash. Gradually stir in a ½ cup of warmed olive oil and salt to taste. Keep skordalia warm, or set aside to cool before refrigerating to reheat when required.
4 Remove lamb from refrigerator 10 minutes before cooking. Heat a barbecue grill or cast-iron pan until medium-hot. Cook lamb for about 4–5 minutes until browned all over and medium-rare. Set fillets aside for 5 minutes.
5 Mix olive paste with extra virgin olive oil. Spread 1 Tbsp circle on each plate, add a dollop of skordalia, slice fillets diagonally and serve atop the paste with green beans on the side.

If you can't find kaffir lime leaves you can use lemon leaves. Just give them a good wash first and pat dry between paper towels. They will give a mild citrus scent to the chicken.

JENNIFER YEE

Kaffir lime chicken kebabs

READY IN: 45 MINUTES
SERVES: 4

Marinade
2 Tbsp fish sauce
2 Tbsp Shao Hsing rice wine (see Glossary, page 173)
2 Tbsp dark soy sauce
zest and juice of 1 lime
2 cloves garlic, crushed
5 slices ginger, finely chopped
1 tsp sesame oil
salt and pepper, to season

Kebabs
8 skinless chicken thigh fillets
48 fresh kaffir lime leaves (see Glossary, page 172), or use lemon leaves
12 bamboo skewers, soaked in warm water for 10-15 minutes

Lime & fish sauce dressing
1 long red chilli, chopped
1 Tbsp wine vinegar
½ cup fish sauce
¼ cup lime juice and zest of 2 limes
1 small carrot, finely julienned, optional
2 cloves garlic, minced
½ cup shaved palm sugar (see Glossary, page 173)
1½ cups warm water, to serve

Herb & lettuce platter
12 buttercrunch or iceberg lettuce leaves
1 small bunch each of mint, coriander and Thai sweet basil leaves (see Glossary, page 173) or use Mediterranean basil
12cm × 22cm diameter round or square rice paper wrappers

1 Place all marinade ingredients in a bowl and mix together until combined.
2 Trim and discard excess fat from chicken. Rinse and pat dry. Cut each into 6 even-sized cubes.
3 Place chicken in a bowl with the marinade ingredients. Toss to combine and leave for 10 minutes. Drain chicken from marinade, reserving this for basting. Wrap a kaffir lime leaf around each piece of chicken and secure onto a skewer. Thread 4 pieces onto each skewer leaving about 1 cm from the pointed end.
4 Heat the barbecue until hot and place skewers on the grill rack. Lay the bare end of the skewers away from the flame. Cook each side for 5 minutes basting several times with the remaining marinade. The chicken is cooked when the juices run clear. Keep the chicken warm.
5 Mix all the dressing ingredients, except the water, together in a bowl, stirring to dissolve the palm sugar. Taste and adjust for saltiness, sourness, sweetness and chilli heat. (The dressing will keep well in the refrigerator.) Dilute the dressing to taste with warm water.
6 Arrange the lettuce, herbs, rice papers and chicken skewers on a large platter. Choose a bowl with slightly wider diameter than the rice paper sheets and fill with warm water.
7 To serve, dip a sheet of rice paper into the water and place this on the plate. Place a lettuce leaf, some herbs and the barbecued chicken (lime leaves removed) on the rice paper and roll to form a cylinder with an open end. Dip the roll into the dressing and eat up.

Taste
food for drinks

Use fresh or frozen broad beans to make this chunky green dip. It can also be made using peas instead of beans. The sour cream, salmon and lime dip is a little luxurious, but easy to make.

LAURIE BLACK

Broad bean & mint dip

READY IN: 15-20 MINUTES
SERVES: 8

500g shelled broad beans, defrosted in the fridge if frozen
1 clove garlic, crushed
1 long green chilli, seeds removed, chopped
juice of 1 lemon
2 Tbsp extra virgin olive oil
2 Tbsp chopped mint

1 Blanch beans in boiling water for 5 minutes if frozen, 10 minutes if fresh. Drain and cool under cold running water. Squeeze each bean from its skin, discarding skins. Mash beans using a fork, mixing in the garlic, chilli and lemon juice, then stir in the oil and mint and season lightly with salt.
2 Cover and refrigerate until required.

COOK'S TIP
• Young green chillies are the least hot of fresh chillies. Once they are sliced and mixed in with other ingredients they will start to release their heat.

Sour cream, salmon & lime dip

READY IN: 8 MINUTES
SERVES: 8

1 clove garlic, crushed
grated zest of 2 limes and juice of 1 lime
250g organic sour cream
250g hot-smoked salmon (see Glossary, page 172), skin and bones discarded
1 tsp chopped dill

1 Place the garlic, lime zest, lime juice, 2 Tbsp sour cream and 2 Tbsp salmon in a food processor and blend. Add the remaining sour cream and pulse to combine.
2 Turn mixture out into a bowl and stir in the remaining salmon and the chopped dill. Season to taste with salt. Cover and refrigerate the dip until it is required.

Delicious morsels from India, pakoras are perfect to have as a nibble in warm weather. Enjoy with beer or pinot gris.

ALLYSON GOFTON

Pakoras with mint dip

READY IN: 30 MINUTES
SERVES: 4

Mint dip
- 1 small to medium red onion, peeled and quartered
- 1 green chilli, seeds removed
- ½ well-packed cup mint leaves
- 1 Tbsp fresh ginger
- 1 cup plain yoghurt

Pakoras
- ¾ cup besan (chickpea) flour
- ½ tsp salt
- ½ tsp cayenne pepper
- 1 tsp turmeric
- ½ tsp ground cumin
- 1 tsp baking powder
- about 1 cup water
- small vegetable pieces, such as green beans, portions of cauliflower and broccoli florets, button mushrooms and eggplant, sliced and quartered
- oil, for frying

1 Prepare the dip by placing the onion, chilli, mint and ginger in a food processor and processing until finely chopped, almost puréed. Add the yoghurt and pulse to combine. Set aside.

2 Sift the besan flour, salt, cayenne, turmeric, cumin and baking powder into a bowl. Add sufficient water to form a smooth batter, the consistency of pouring cream.

3 Blanch the beans, cauliflower and broccoli in boiling water for 1 minute. Refresh in cold water. Pat vegetables dry with a paper towel. Wipe the mushrooms. Quickly pan-fry the eggplant.

4 Dip dry vegetable portions in the batter. Deep-fry until crisp and golden. Transfer to an absorbent paper towel to drain off the excess fat. Serve with mint dip.

COOK'S TIP
• When buying besan flour, look for stoneground — it's sold in most health food shops and gives a wonderful texture.

Tramezzini are little crustless Italian sandwiches that you see everywhere in Italy from curbside cafes to bars. They're always a hot-seller for afternoon tea at home, too.

LAURIE BLACK

Smoked paprika & prawn tramezzini

READY IN: 10 MINUTES
MAKES: 16

24 raw, peeled prawns
1 cup good-quality mayonnaise, such as Best Foods or Kato
juice of ½ lemon
1 Tbsp roughly chopped parsley
8 slices day-old white bread, crusts removed
smoked paprika

1 Put all the prawns in a large pot of boiling water, stir once and cook for 1–2 minutes until they have turned pink and are no longer translucent. Drain and cool quickly under cold water. Drain again and keep in the refrigerator until required.
2 Chop the prawns into 1cm chunks. Mix the mayonnaise with the lemon juice and stir in the prawns and parsley.
3 Arrange 4 of the bread slices on a board. Spread each with a generous amount of prawn mayonnaise, almost to the edges. Sprinkle a pinch of smoked paprika over each sandwich then place remaining slices of bread on top, pressing down lightly. (Sandwiches can be wrapped and kept in the fridge for several hours at this stage if necessary.) Using a sharp bread knife cut each sandwich into quarters and serve.

Thinly sliced cold veal in creamy tuna mayonnaise topped with capers — a delicious Italian antipasto dish.

LAURIE BLACK

Vitello tonnato

READY IN: BEST PREPARED A DAY IN ADVANCE
SERVES: 10 AS PART OF A LIGHT LUNCH OR ANTIPASTO

Veal
800g–1kg veal top rump, in one piece
½ cup white wine
½ leek
½ carrot, split
1 parsley stem
1 bayleaf
4 black peppercorns

Tuna mayonnaise
185g can of tuna in olive oil (or vegetable oil)
4 Tbsp capers
6 small anchovies
4 Tbsp lemon juice
150ml olive oil
250ml good quality mayonnaise

To serve
extra capers
fresh bread

1 Place veal in a saucepan and cover meat well with cold water to establish how much is needed. Remove veal to a plate and add wine, leek, carrot, parsley, bayleaf and peppercorns to the water. This is called a court bouillon (see Glossary, page 172). Bring to the boil, add the veal to the saucepan, adjust heat so that bouillon just simmers, and cover saucepan with lid. Simmer meat for 1 hour, checking from time to time that the bouillon is simmering gently. Turn heat off and leave meat in bouillon for 1 hour as it cools. Remove meat and refrigerate for at least 3 hours. Strain bouillon, discarding solids. Keep bouillon as a base for a soup or risotto.

2 Meanwhile, make the sauce by placing the tuna, capers and anchovies in a food processor. Add 1 Tbsp of lemon juice and blend until smooth. With the motor running, gradually add olive oil in a thin stream. Finally add remaining lemon juice and blend again. Place mayonnaise in a mixing bowl and gradually whisk in the tuna mixture until well-combined. Refrigerate sauce for at least 3 hours.

3 When veal is well-chilled, use a very sharp knife to slice it as thinly as possible (slice widthwise, as with a loaf of bread). Spread a layer of sauce on a serving platter and top with overlapping slices of veal. Spread with more sauce and repeat until veal is all used. Finish with a generous layer of sauce, smoothing with a palette knife or spatula. Cover platter loosely with foil, trying to keep it from touching the sauce, and refrigerate for at least 6 hours.

4 Sprinkle more capers over the platter. Serve vitello tonnato with fresh bread and freshly ground black pepper.

COOK'S TIP
• Pre-order the veal and ask your butcher to trim off any sinew or silverskin.

Marinating raw fish in lemon or lime juice 'cooks' the fish — acids in the juice cause the flesh to whiten. The longer you marinate the fish, the more the flavour develops.

TRACEY SUNDERLAND

Snapper & shrimp ceviche

READY IN: 1 HOUR 25 MINUTES
SERVES: 4

300g snapper fillets, skinned and boned
¾ cup freshly squeezed lemon or lime juice
300g shrimp, defrosted (see Cook's Tips)
1 green chilli, seeds in and finely chopped
2 spring onions, finely sliced
4 tomatoes, cored, seeded and diced
2 Tbsp parsley, finely chopped
1 Tbsp coriander, finely chopped
½ tsp sugar
blue taco chips, to serve

1 Cut the snapper into approximately 1cm cubes and place in a ceramic or glass bowl. Pour the lemon or lime juice (you can use a mix of both) over the top, cover and refrigerate for 1 hour to marinate.
2 Place the shrimp in a sieve and shake away any remaining ice. Tip onto paper towels and pat dry. Add the shrimp to the snapper after the fish has marinated. Then stir through the remaining ingredients and leave for 10 minutes. Season to taste with sea salt and freshly ground black pepper.
3 To serve, use a slotted spoon to place in medium-sized glass bowls. Scoop up the spicy seafood with blue taco chips. You could also serve this on top of crunchy salad greens.

COOK'S TIPS
- Buy the freshest fish you can find when preparing ceviche and use it the same day. Frozen fish will not be nice for this dish, but frozen shrimp (which are cooked before freezing) are perfect.
- Shrimp defrost very quickly, so take them out an hour or so before you plan to use them and leave them in a bowl to defrost.
- Small prawns could also be used for this ceviche recipe, but make sure they are precooked.

Bonita, an excellent tapas bar in Ponsonby, Auckland, is already well-known for its dish of sausages in red wine. Here's our version.

LAURIE BLACK

Sausages in red wine with red onion, rosemary & parsley

READY IN: 20 MINUTES (ONION MIX CAN BE COOKED IN ADVANCE)
SERVES: 4

- 2 tsp olive oil
- 1 medium red onion, cut into 8 wedges
- 1 clove garlic, crushed
- 2 sprigs rosemary
- 1 lemon wedge
- 2 tsp brown sugar
- ¾ cup red wine
- 12 tiny breakfast sausages, preferably pork
- 1 Tbsp chopped flat leaf parsley, to serve

1 Heat oil in a frying pan to medium heat and add red onion, garlic, rosemary and a good squeeze of lemon juice. Cook, stirring until onion softens but isn't browning. Add sugar and ½ cup red wine, simmer for 2 minutes then set aside.

2 In another pan, cook the sausages, turning frequently, until brown all over. Add onion and wine mixture to pan along with remaining wine and a pinch of salt and simmer for a few minutes. Serve sausages in the pan, or transfer to individual pans if you have them. Scatter parsley over the top.

This hearty nibble is ideal over summer when we need substantial bites that are healthy, easy to make and interesting.
ALLYSON GOFTON

Indian-spiked potato kebabs with tomato & lime dip

READY IN: 30 MINUTES
SERVES: 10 AS A NIBBLE

Dip
oil
1 tsp cumin seeds
¼ tsp turmeric
¼ tsp chilli paste
1 tsp minced garlic
1 tsp minced ginger
3 large tomatoes, blanched and peeled (or 400g can tomatoes in purée or juice)
grated rind and juice of 1 lime
1 Tbsp chopped fresh coriander
extra chopped fresh coriander, to garnish

Potatoes
750g baby new-season potatoes, scrubbed
oil, to fry
1 tsp cumin seeds
1–2 Tbsp Indian curry paste (use your favourite)
¼ cup water
1 Tbsp chopped fresh coriander

1 To make the dip, heat a dash of oil in a medium-sized pan and add the cumin seeds. Cook for 30 seconds then add the turmeric, chilli paste, garlic and ginger. Cook for 1–2 minutes, until the mix is fragrant.
2 Dice the peeled tomatoes and add with the lime rind and juice. Cover and cook for a further 3–4 minutes. Season to taste with a pinch of salt and sugar.
3 Place the tomato mixture in a food processor with the coriander and process until smooth. Set aside until needed.
4 Cook the potatoes in boiling, salted water until just tender. Drain.
5 Heat a dash of oil in a large pan and add the cumin seeds. Cook for 30 seconds until fragrant and then add the curry paste and potatoes and toss gently for 1–2 minutes. Add the water and cook, tossing the potatoes in the pan until they are coated in the paste.
6 Serve on skewers or with toothpicks. Garnish with the extra coriander and accompany with the warm (or cold, if preferred) tomato and lime dipping sauce.

These tasty filled tortillas make a quick and easy finger food.

TRACEY SUNDERLAND

Potato & smoked cheese quesadillas

READY IN: 25 MINUTES
SERVES: 4

- 2 large potatoes, cleaned but not peeled
- 1 tsp salt
- 8 fresh sun-dried tomato tortillas (such as Quality Bakers)
- 1 red onion, finely sliced
- 300g can butter beans, drained
- 1 red chilli, finely sliced
- 1½ cups grated, smoked cheddar cheese
- 1 green pepper, ends and seeds removed, finely diced
- 3 tomatoes, finely diced
- 1½ cups grated colby cheese
- sour cream, to serve

1 Put potatoes in a saucepan, cover with cold water and bring to the boil. Add salt and simmer for 12–15 minutes until potatoes are tender. Drain and place saucepan under a cold running tap for 1 minute. Leave the cooked potatoes to sit in the water for a further minute until they are cool enough to peel. Peel and grate immediately, season and mix through with your fingers.
2 Heat a large frying pan or grill plate until medium-hot. You may prefer to use a flat barbecue plate, as you will be able to heat 2 tortillas at once. Warm one side of a flour tortilla, until it begins to show air bubbles, then remove. Warm another tortilla through on one side, then turn it over to heat. This tortilla will be the base of a quesadilla.
3 While still in the pan, add to this tortilla a quarter of the grated potato and onion, 2 Tbsp butter beans and a little chilli. Sprinkle with some smoked cheddar, add some green pepper and tomato then cover with the colby cheese and season well with salt and pepper. Top with the first pre-warmed tortilla, placing the browned side on top of the ingredients. Be careful not to add too much filling. Now carefully flip the whole quesadilla over to cook the other side and melt the cheese.
4 Continue to warm the quesadilla through, adjusting the heat if necessary until the cheese is melted. Repeat until you have 4 quesadillas. Cut into wedges and enjoy with sour cream and a light crispy salad on the side.

COOK'S TIP
- Take care when slicing chillies — don't touch your eyes or any sensitive skin with hands that have been in contact with chilli.

Nachos are a versatile and easy classic. This meat-free variation is ideal to serve with drinks.

TRACEY SUNDERLAND

Refried-bean nachos with guacamole

READY IN: 25 MINUTES
SERVES: 4

Refried-bean dip
2 Tbsp oil
3 spring onions, finely diced
1 red chilli, finely sliced
2 cloves garlic, crushed
3 tomatoes, core removed, diced
400g can refried beans
1 cup grated tasty cheese
natural salted tortilla chips
1 punnet cherry tomatoes, halved
2 fresh green chillies, finely sliced
2 cups grated mozzarella

Guacamole
2 avocados, diced
½ small onion, finely diced
1 Tbsp chopped coriander
juice of 2 limes, or 1 lemon
shake of Tabasco
2 Tbsp chopped parsley or coriander, to serve

1 Heat a heavy-based frying pan to a medium heat and add oil. Sauté spring onion, chilli and garlic for 2 minutes. Add tomatoes and simmer for 7 minutes. Stir in refried beans and cheese and simmer for 4–5 minutes. Season to taste.
2 Choose a large ovenproof baking dish or make individual bowls of nachos on earthenware or tin plates. Scatter tortilla chips over the base and spoon on the refried bean dip randomly. Scatter cherry tomatoes, green chilli and mozzarella over the chips.
3 Repeat and finish with a good layer of extra mozzarella on top. Place under a grill, preheated to 200°C, for 10 minutes or until cheese is melted.
4 For the guacamole, toss the ingredients together in a bowl and mash roughly with a fork. Season to taste.
5 Sprinkle nachos with chopped parsley or coriander and spoon guacamole on top or serve on the side.

COOK'S TIPS
• The refried bean dip will freeze well in a small sealed container.
• If you are serving guacamole on its own, add a small diced tomato and half a clove of garlic, finely mashed — they have been omitted here due to the other flavours in the dish. Coriander can also be omitted.

These crispy pumpkin chips are delicious served up with Thai curry or served alongside grilled chicken or beef scented with plenty of garlic.

ALLYSON GOFTON

Thai-spiced pumpkin chips with minted sour cream

READY IN: 30 MINUTES
SERVES: 4

Pumpkin chips
1kg butternut pumpkin
1 Tbsp Thai red-curry paste
¼ cup oil or softened butter
2 Tbsp honey

Minted sour cream
2 Tbsp chopped fresh mint
½ cup sour cream
lime juice, optional

1 Cut the butternut pumpkin into 2cm-thick slices. Cut each slice into triangular wedges and place in a large bowl.
2 Mix together the curry paste, oil or butter and honey to make a smooth paste. Toss the pumpkin in the mix. Season with salt and freshly ground black pepper. Place in a single layer on a baking paper-lined tray.
3 Place the tray at the top of an oven preheated to 200°C (fanbake) for about 15 minutes until cooked.
4 For the minted sour cream, mix the mint and sour cream together and season with a squeeze of lime juice, if you wish. Try fresh coriander or chives if you don't have mint. Serve with the pumpkin chips.

COOK'S TIP
• Butternut pumpkins are ideal to halve and bake with just a knob of butter and some salt and freshly ground black pepper.

Taste
baking

This cake is absolutely delicious and the lemon syrup adds a sweet tang. Using almond liqueur for the syrup enhances the flavour the marzipan offers.

ALLYSON GOFTON

Citrus & almond cake

READY IN: 1 HOUR 15 MINUTES
SERVES: 10

Cake
- 175g butter
- 1 cup caster sugar
- 1 Tbsp finely grated lemon or orange rind
- 3 eggs, beaten
- 1 tsp almond essence
- ½ cup sour cream
- 2 cups flour
- 3 tsp baking powder
- ½ cup fresh lemon juice
- 50–100g marzipan, finely diced
- ½ cup unblanched almonds

Lemon syrup
- ¼ cup caster sugar
- ¼ cup fresh lemon juice
- ¼ cup almond liqueur

1 Beat the butter, sugar and lemon rind together, until light and fluffy.
2 Add eggs one at a time, beating well after each addition. Beat in the almond essence and sour cream.
3 Sift together the flour and baking powder and fold into the creamed mixture with lemon juice and marzipan. Turn into a well-greased and lined 14cm × 20cm loaf tin. Arrange the almonds on top.
4 Cook at 170°C for 1 hour, or until well risen, golden and an inserted skewer comes out clean.
5 Meanwhile, make the lemon syrup. Dissolve the sugar in the lemon juice and almond liqueur over a low heat and boil rapidly for 2–3 minutes.
6 Spoon the warm lemon syrup over the hot, cooked loaf, then allow the cake to cool and absorb the syrup before turning out to cool thoroughly. Serve warm, or cold if it lasts that long!

This one-rise bread has a lovely softness and malty taste from the treacle. Linseeds add a wonderful nutty texture, not to mention a healthy touch.

ALLYSON GOFTON

Basic one-rise bread

READY IN: 2 HOURS
MAKES: 1 LOAF

1¼ tsp dried yeast or 4 tsp Surebake yeast
1 cup warm water
1 tsp sugar
1½ cups high-grade flour
1½ cups wholemeal flour
1 tsp salt
2 Tbsp milk powder, optional
50g butter, softened
½ cup linseeds, or sunflower seeds, or pumpkin seeds
2 Tbsp treacle or golden syrup
extra warm water

Toppings
beaten egg or milk, to glaze
2 Tbsp linseeds, or oat flakes, oat bran, pumpkin seeds or sunflower seeds (or a mixture of these)

1 Stir yeast into the warm water and sugar and set aside for 15 minutes until frothy.
2 Put high-grade and wholemeal flour, salt and milk powder (if using) into a processor and pulse to sift. Add the butter and process until rubbed in. Pulse in the seeds.
3 Add the treacle to the frothy yeast mixture and, with the motor running, pour the liquid down the feed tube as fast as the flour can absorb it and process to a very soft dough. Add any extra water if required. The mixture should be soft but not tacky. Process for no more than 1 minute.
4 Turn the mixture out onto a lightly floured board and knead lightly. Press out to a 20cm × 10cm rectangle and roll up tightly from the long side. Transfer to a well-greased 20cm loaf tin. Cover with greased plastic wrap and set aside for 1 hour in a warm place until the dough doubles in bulk. As a guide, it should rise to the level of the top of the tin. Brush with beaten egg or milk to glaze and sprinkle with extra seeds.
5 Bake at 200°C for 30–35 minutes or until the loaf sounds hollow when tapped underneath. Remove from the oven, turn out immediately onto a cake rack and leave to cool.

COOK'S TIPS
• To make by hand, 'sponge' the yeast as described in step 1 and add the treacle. Sift the flour, salt and milk powder into a bowl. Rub in the butter and stir through the linseeds. Make a well in the centre and gradually pour in the frothy yeast mixture. Once most of the flour has been absorbed turn the dough out onto a lightly floured board and knead well for 10 minutes until the dough is smooth. Continue from step 4.
• To make in a breadmaker, place the ingredients in the breadmaker in this order: water, butter, treacle, salt, flours, linseeds, milk powder, sugar and yeast. Set the machine for 'quick bread'.

A twist on an old favourite, shortbread is my favourite all-year-round biscuit.

ALLYSON GOFTON

Brown-sugar shortbread

READY IN: 1 HOUR
MAKES: 24–30 PIECES

250g butter
½ cup firmly packed soft brown sugar
1¾ cups flour
½ cup rice flour, cornflour or plain flour
½ tsp salt

1 Beat the butter and brown sugar together until light and creamy.
2 Sift the flour, rice flour (cornflour or flour) and salt together and work into the creamed mixture.
3 Turn the mixture out onto a floured board and knead together. Roll the dough out to 1–1.5cm thickness and cut into rounds. Place on a greased baking tray and prick the top of each three times with the tines of a fork.
4 Bake at 160°C for 20–25 minutes or until firm to the touch and the biscuits are beginning to become a light brown around the edges. Cool on the tray for 10 minutes before transferring to a cake rack to cool completely. Store in an airtight container.

COOK'S TIP
- Top with an almond, half a pecan or walnut, or try halved glacé cherries.

This is my favourite cake. The flavour is simple and comforting and it is best served warm, cut in wedges and spread with a little butter.

ALLYSON GOFTON

Mum's tea cake

READY IN: 1 HOUR
MAKES: 20CM ROUND CAKE

Cake
50g butter, softened
¾ cup caster sugar
1 egg
1½ cups flour
2 tsp baking powder
¾ cup milk

Topping
1 Tbsp butter, softened
2 Tbsp extra caster sugar
½ tsp cinnamon

1 Mix the butter and sugar together in a bowl with a wooden spoon. There is not enough here to cream so mix it as well as you can. Beat in the egg.
2 Sift the flour and baking powder and fold into the butter mixture alternately with the milk.
3 Spoon the batter into a well-greased and floured or paper-lined 20cm round cake tin and bake at 180°C for 40 minutes.
4 Allow the cake to stand in the tin for 5 minutes, before turning it out onto a cake rack. You need to allow this time before turning out as the freshly cooked cake will be too tender and is likely to break in the process.
5 While the cake is still hot, spread the top with the extra butter and sprinkle the sugar and cinnamon over the top.

These stylish scones are ideal to serve as part of an afternoon tea with friends.

LAURIE BLACK

Gruyère & pecan scones

READY IN: 20 MINUTES
MAKES: 12

3 cups flour
4 tsp baking powder
¼ tsp salt
50g butter, chilled and diced
¼ cup roughly chopped pecans
2 cups grated gruyère cheese
1-1½ cups milk
butter, for serving
scone-sized squares of sliced ham, for serving

1 Place flour, baking powder and salt in food processor and pulse to combine. Add chilled butter and process until texture is sandy. Transfer to a large mixing bowl.
2 Stir in pecans and ½ cup of the cheese. Using a dinner knife, mix in enough milk to form a soft dough. Turn the dough out onto a floured work surface, knead lightly and pat into a 3cm-thick square. Using a sharp knife, cut into 12 even scones and transfer these to a baking tray lined with baking paper. Top with remaining cheese.
3 Bake at 210°C for 12–15 minutes until firm. Cool briefly on a rack and serve, split, with butter and ham.

COOK'S TIP
- Over-mixing will result in a tough texture. Only mix together until just combined.

This is Louise cake with extras: extra coconut, extra raspberries on top of the jam and extra-rich pastry at the bottom. All you need is a nice cup of tea to go with it.

LAURIE BLACK

Super-duper Louise cake

READY IN: 55 MINUTES
MAKES: 15 PORTIONS

Base
125g butter
4 Tbsp caster sugar
4 eggs, separated
1¾ cups flour
1½ tsp baking powder

Topping
½ cup raspberry jam
1 cup frozen raspberries
¾ cup sugar
2 cups strand coconut

1 Cream butter and caster sugar until pale and light. Beat in yolks, one at a time.
2 Sift flour and baking powder together and add to butter mixture in three batches. When mixture becomes too dry to combine, turn out onto a clean work surface and gently knead it together with your hands. Press it evenly into the bottom of a 19cm × 28cm baking tray neatly lined with baking paper.
3 Spread jam over the pastry, then scatter raspberries over the top.
4 Beat egg whites in a large clean bowl until stiff peaks form. Using a large metal spoon, gently fold in the sugar and coconut in several batches, until just combined. Gently spread this meringue mixture over the raspberries.
5 Bake at 180°C for 40 minutes until the meringue is light but firm to the touch — you may need to loosely cover it with foil after about 25 minutes cooking time if the top is already browning. Cool on a rack. Cut into squares to serve.

COOK'S TIP
• Be gentle when folding ingredients together — you don't want to knock out all the air you've just beaten into the meringue.

Use hazelnut, almond or walnut oil to make these deliciously crispy, nutty biscuits.

ALLYSON GOFTON

Hazelnut biscuits

READY IN: 40 MINUTES
MAKES: 30

1 cup hazelnut oil
¾ cup sugar
1 egg
2 cups flour
1 tsp baking powder
¼ cup finely chopped toasted hazelnuts
about 15 hazelnuts, halved

1 Mix the hazelnut oil, sugar and egg together in a bowl.
2 Sift the flour and baking powder together and stir into the wet mixture along with the finely chopped hazelnuts.
3 Roll heaped teaspoonfuls of the mixture into balls and place on a greased baking tray. Place a halved hazelnut into the centre of each biscuit.
4 Bake at 160°C for 15–20 minutes until lightly golden. Cool on a cake rack. Store in an airtight container.

COOK'S TIP
• Nut oils can be expensive — you can use half hazelnut oil and half plain-tasting oil, such as canola.

A real smooth operator, versatile lemon curd glides easily from breakfast to dessert.

LAURIE BLACK

Laurie's lemon curd

READY IN: 20 MINUTES
MAKES: 2¾ CUPS

Peel from 4 lemons, removed using a vegetable peeler, white pith scraped off
300ml freshly squeezed lemon juice
150g unsalted butter, diced
250g caster sugar
2 eggs
6 egg yolks

1 Combine all ingredients in a generously sized heatproof bowl and place over a saucepan of not-quite-simmering water, ensuring the water does not come up to the bottom of the bowl.
2 Stir gently as the curd cooks and scrape the bowl every few minutes using a rubber spatula.
3 When the curd starts to thicken, strain into a bowl and press a piece of paper onto the surface to prevent a skin from forming.
4 Cool and transfer to clean jars and refrigerate. It will keep refrigerated for about 2 weeks.

VELVETY VARIATIONS
• Lime curd is the easiest variation on lemon curd. Just replace lemon juice and peel with lime juice and peel.
• Orange curd is just the thing to make when New Zealand navel oranges are in season. Replace 200ml of the juice with orange juice, making up the rest with lemon juice. Replace all the lemon peel with orange peel, again taking care to remove white pith.
• Passionfruit curd might be the best of all. Reduce the amount of lemon juice by 100ml and add 150ml fresh passionfruit pulp. Use orange peel instead of lemon as it enhances the passionfruit flavour.
• Hot-pink raspberry curd has a startling appearance that I love. Cook about 2 cups of raspberries (frozen berries are quite suitable) with 1 Tbsp water until they collapse, purée in a blender and strain to remove seeds. Use 250ml raspberry purée and 50ml lemon juice, omitting the peel.
• If you're a pastry maker, try making the little meringue tarts (see page 136) with chocolate pastry, replacing the lime curd with raspberry. Serve with vanilla ice cream and a little chocolate sauce.

COOK'S TIP
• For satiny curd, stir the mixture continuously as it cooks and scrape the bowl often with a rubber spatula.

You can't use true curd in large lemon meringue pies as it isn't stable enough to heat up. But these tarts cook so quickly the curd barely increases in temperature and they always look impressive.

LAURIE BLACK

Little lime curd meringue tarts

MAKES: 6 SMALL TARTS

6 small tart shells made using homemade or
   bought short sweet pastry, baked blind
   (see Glossary, page 172)
lime curd, chilled
3 egg whites
½ cup caster sugar

1 Fill tart shells with lime curd (see Velvety Variations, page 134).
2 To make the meringue, beat 3 egg whites to stiff peaks. Add the caster sugar in 1 Tbsp amounts, beating each time until smooth and glossy.
3 Spoon meringue over the curd in the tart shells. Be sure to seal the edges of the tart with meringue.
4 Bake for 3–4 minutes at 220°C, just until meringue is tinged with brown.

Use chocolate chips for these wicked biscuits, which will keep well in an airtight container.

ALLYSON GOFTON

Toll house biscuits

READY IN: 1–1½ HOURS
MAKES: 30

175g butter
¾ cup brown sugar
¾ cup caster sugar
2 eggs
2¼ cups flour
1 tsp baking powder
2 cups chocolate chips

1 Beat the butter and sugars together until light and creamy. Add the eggs one at a time, beating well after each addition.
2 Sift the flour and baking powder evenly over the creamed mixture. Sprinkle the chocolate chips over and fold together.
3 Place heaped tablespoonfuls of the mixture onto a greased baking tray, leaving room for the biscuits to spread.
4 Bake at 180°C for 20 minutes, or until the biscuits are beginning to lightly brown and are firm to the touch. Transfer to a cake rack to cool.

COOK'S TIP
• You can use chocolate bits in this recipe but do not use chocolate hail as it will melt.

Brownies seem to be taking over from our favourite muffins. This one, if cooked to squidgy, is absolutely to die for and ideal to serve with coffee for friends.

ALLYSON GOFTON

White chocolate brownies

READY IN: 2 HOURS
MAKES: 24–30 PIECES

Brownies
275g white chocolate, roughly chopped
250g butter
1 cup caster sugar
4 eggs
1 Tbsp vanilla essence
2 cups flour
1 cup chopped pecans, preferably toasted

Icing
100g butter, softened
1½ cups icing sugar
few drops vanilla essence
1–2 Tbsp milk

1 Put the chocolate pieces in the top of a double saucepan with the butter. Warm over boiling water until just melted. This can be done in the microwave allowing about 2–3 minutes on high power. Be careful not to overcook the chocolate, as it will burn easily. Cool.
2 Beat together the sugar, eggs and vanilla essence until the mixture is light and fluffy.
3 Sift the flour and fold into the chocolate and butter mixture alternately with the egg mixture and pecans.
4 Turn into a greased, floured and lined 23–25cm square cake tin.
5 Bake at 160°C for 40–45 minutes until the top is lightly golden but the centre is still a little soft. Remove from the oven and cool to room temperature before refrigerating for 3–4 hours. Remove from the tin.
6 To make the icing, beat the butter until pale and fluffy. Sift the icing sugar and beat into the creamed butter with the vanilla essence and sufficient milk until you have a fluffy, light mixture. If you need the mixture to spread more easily, add a little more milk.
7 Ice the cake. Cut into squares to serve.
8 Dust with cocoa or decorate with melted chocolate.

COOK'S TIP
- Good-quality white chocolate is made entirely from cocoa butter. Read the label to check for this. Usually, price will be an indicator of quality.

What's not to love about flaky light pastry, crunchy with sugar, and a tart apple filling? You'll need to allow at least two of these per person.

LAURIE BLACK

Small apple cinnamon turnovers

READY IN: 1½ HOURS
SERVES: 10–12

3 medium Granny Smith apples, peeled and cored
5 tsp sugar
¾ tsp cinnamon
1 Tbsp lemon juice
4 Tbsp water
400g flaky puff pastry, defrosted
1 Tbsp milk
2 Tbsp extra sugar

1 Dice apples and place in a small saucepan with sugar, cinnamon, lemon juice and water. Stir once to combine, then cover pan, place over a medium heat and cook for 5 minutes, stirring once more, until apple is very soft. Set apple aside to cool.
2 Roll pastry out to 4mm thickness on a floured work surface. Cut out 10–12 circles of 10cm diameter. Place a heaped tablespoon of apple on one half of each circle, leaving 5mm clear at the edge. Wet your fingertip and run it around the edge of each pastry circle to make a damp ring, then fold pastry over apple and press and crimp to seal edges.
3 Space turnovers on a baking paper-lined baking sheet. Refrigerate for 15 minutes (or overnight, if you wish to bake them first thing in the morning).
4 Carefully brush the top of each turnover with a little milk and sprinkle evenly with the extra sugar. Brush any spilt sugar off the paper. Bake at 200°C for 10–15 minutes until golden. Cool before serving. Keep cold turnovers in an airtight container for up to 1 day.

COOK'S TIP
• Puff pastry is carefully layered as it is made, which produces the flaky layers once it is cooked. Because of this, you cannot roll offcuts together into a ball and roll pastry out again, so you need to keep your circles as close together as possible when cutting them out. You have to get them all right the first time!

The fruit hides inside a rich almond butter encased in crisp buttery layers of filo.

ALLYSON GOFTON

Blueberry turnovers

READY IN: 40 MINUTES
MAKES: 6

125g softened butter
200g marzipan (buy Odense from New World supermarkets)
2 eggs
¼ cup flour
12 sheets filo pastry (see Glossary, page 172)
125–150g butter, melted
1 punnet blueberries

1 Beat the butter, marzipan, eggs and flour together until smooth.
2 Take 1 sheet of filo pastry, brush with butter, place a second sheet on top and brush with butter. Fold in half lengthwise. Place a large spoonful of almond mixture onto the top of the right-hand corner and place a few blueberries on top.
3 Fold over to make a triangle and enclose the filling. Continue to fold down the length of the filo to make a triangle that completely encloses the filling. Fold over any excess pastry onto the triangle. Brush with butter and place on a greased baking tray. Repeat this process until you have 6 identical triangles.
4 Bake the turnovers at 200°C for 20 minutes until well risen and golden.
5 Dust with icing sugar and serve hot with whipped cream.

COOK'S TIP
- To stop filo pastry from drying out, cover it with a clean damp tea towel.

PHOTOGRAPH BY ALAN GILLARD

Molasses sugar, dark rum, ginger and citrus fruits make this gingerbread particularly good.

ALLYSON GOFTON

Barbados gingerbread

READY IN: 1 HOUR 50 MINUTES
SERVES: 10

250g butter
1 cup molasses sugar, firmly packed
½ cup dark rum
¾ cup full-cream milk
½ cup good-quality marmalade
2 size-7 eggs, beaten
grated rind 2 lemons, 2 oranges and 2 limes
3 cups flour
2 tsp baking soda
1½ tsp baking powder
1½–2 Tbsp ground ginger
2 tsp ground cinnamon
1 tsp grated nutmeg
1 tsp ground cardamom
½ tsp ground cloves
150g packet crystallised ginger, finely sliced
¼ cup lemon and orange peel

1 Melt together butter and molasses sugar, stirring to make a smooth mixture of the 2 ingredients. Remove from heat and stir in the rum, milk, marmalade, eggs and grated rinds. Set aside to cool.
2 Into a large bowl sift together flour, baking soda, baking powder and spices and make a well in the centre.
3 Slowly pour in melted mixture, stirring all the time to form a smooth batter. Beat in ¾ of the crystallised ginger and all the peel.
4 Pour into a greased, baking paper-lined 23–24cm square cake tin and sprinkle with remaining crystallised ginger.
5 Bake at 180°C for 1½ hours until well risen and firm to the touch. Cool in the tin.

COOK'S TIP
• This tastes better if kept wrapped in an airtight container for 2 days before eating. Serve in slices, buttered or unbuttered.

Taste
desserts

This is an impressively simple, melt-in-the-mouth dessert. I love the pinky-red colours of raspberries and rose Turkish delight with this pile of crisp, light, vanilla meringues.

LAURIE BLACK

Rose & raspberry meringues with cream

READY IN: 3¾ HOURS (MERINGUES BEST MADE AT LEAST ½ DAY PRIOR)
SERVES: 8–10 (22 MERINGUES)

- 2 egg whites
- ½ cup caster sugar
- ¼ tsp pure vanilla essence, or ½ tsp raspberry essence, optional
- ½ cup cream
- 4 pieces rose Turkish delight, each sliced in 4
- ½ cup raspberries
- 3 Tbsp icing sugar

1 Place egg whites in a very clean mixer bowl and whisk until glossy and white with tiny bubbles. Add one third of the sugar and beat for 4 minutes on high speed. Add another third of sugar and whisk for another 4 minutes. Add remaining sugar and beat for 3 minutes. Add essence and beat for 10–20 seconds until well-combined. Mixture should now be satiny white and very stiff.
2 Scrape meringue off whisk and add back to the bowl. Don't bang the bowl as this will knock air out of the mixture. Scoop balls of meringue using a smallish dessertspoon and tip them carefully onto trays lined with baking paper. Use the back of another spoon to push the meringue into place. Bake at 115°C for 1½ hours, turning trays once to ensure even colouration. Turn oven off and leave trays inside to cool for 1 hour. Remove trays to racks and leave until meringues are cold. Store in paper-lined, airtight containers until required.
3 To assemble, whip cream to medium stiffness. Spread a little cream in a 15cm-diameter circle on a flat serving plate. Arrange a layer of meringues on top, then dab a little more cream into gaps between meringues. Stack more meringues on top, in a slightly smaller circle. Add more cream to any gaps and add more meringues until you have used them all. Dot cream pockets with raspberries and Turkish delight, scattering remaining berries on the plate. Sift icing sugar over the top just before serving. Serve within 10 minutes of making.

COOK'S TIP
- Feel free to put your own interpretation on this dessert. You could sprinkle halved, toasted hazelnuts onto the pockets of cream and grate over some dark chocolate or add ½ teaspoon grated lemon rind to the cream and decorate with chopped pistachio nuts and candied peel.

This is a classic, berry-red English summer pudding.

LAURIE BLACK

Summer pudding

READY IN: 2 DAYS
SERVES: 6–8

10 cups mixed fresh berries (raspberries, blueberries, boysenberries, blackberries, currants — but NO strawberries)
½ cup caster sugar
1 cup water
1 loaf sliced white bread, 1–2 days old
cream, to serve

1 Mix all the berries together and place in a large pan – one with a glass lid is best. Sprinkle sugar over berries, then add the water to the pan. Cover and place over a medium-high heat. Cook for 3 minutes then check to see if mixture is nearing a boil. Stir once and cover again, cooking for another 2 minutes, or until the whole pan has just boiled. Set aside to cool.
2 Trim crusts from the bread and cut a circle from 1 slice to line the base of a 7-cup capacity pudding bowl (or use 6–8 small bowls, or a glass terrine dish, if you prefer). Cut triangles or rectangles from more bread and carefully fit pieces into the bowl to line it snugly. Have more pieces of bread ready to cover the top.
3 Carefully spoon berry mixture into the bowl to fill it completely, using a slotted spoon for the final ⅓ so that some syrup is left in the pan.
4 Once berry mixture has filled the bowl, cover top of pudding with more bread fitted snugly together. Spoon some more berry syrup over the top, then put any remaining syrup in a container to refrigerate until serving. Cover pudding with plastic wrap and weight carefully with 2 or 3 plates and a full can (for example, of tinned tomatoes) on top. Refrigerate for at least 2 days before serving. (Best eaten within 5 days.)
5 Serve by spooning directly from the bowl, or turning the pudding out carefully onto a serving plate. Small puddings can be served whole, and a summer pudding made in a terrine dish can be turned out, then sliced.
6 Serve with more fresh berries, remaining berry syrup, and cream.

COOK'S TIPS
- Make sure the bread is stale, not squishy and fresh. Fresh bread turns slimy.
- Make plenty of berry compote so your pudding is fat with berries and soaked in juice. Any excess compote is perfect for spooning over the pudding when serving.

Deep ruby-red cherries are a special treat, so stretch them with sliced apples to make this homely, yet attractive, pie. Using bought frozen, sweet short pastry makes the task easier.

ALLYSON GOFTON

Cherry & apple pie

READY IN: 60–80 MINUTES
SERVES: 4–6

300g packet frozen cherries, defrosted
2 Tbsp water
2 medium-sized eating apples, peeled and sliced
1 Tbsp cornflour
dash of kirsch, optional (see Glossary, page 173)
600g sweet short pastry, defrosted
1 egg, beaten

1 Place the frozen cherries into a saucepan with the water and poach just until the cherries are warm. Use a slotted spoon to lift the cherries from the liquid. Set aside. Add finely sliced apples to the cooking liquid and cook for 5 minutes until the slices are tender.
2 Dissolve the cornflour in a dash of water or kirsch, add to the saucepan and cook until thickened. Remove from the heat, add the cherries and cool.
3 Cut pastry block almost in half, making one piece a little larger than the other. Roll out the larger portion so it covers the base and sides of a 23cm shallow pie dish. Trim the edges and refrigerate.
4 Roll out the second block of pastry to 3mm thickness. Rest it for 5 minutes before cutting into 2cm-wide strips. You will need about 12 strips, but the number required will depend on how close you wish to make your basket-weave top.
5 Brush the edge of the pastry with beaten egg. Fill the centre with the cooled cherry and apple mixture. Place sufficient strips across the top of the pastry dish so they almost touch. From the left-hand side, press just one strip of pastry onto the edge and weave it over and under the pastry strips placed along the top edge. Repeat this process, ensuring the strips alternate being over and under. Trim the edges and brush the top of the pie with egg wash.
6 Bake at 200°C in the middle of the oven for 10 minutes. Cover with baking paper and then lower the temperature to 180°C for a further 20 minutes, or until the pastry is golden brown and the cherry sauce is bubbling through the top. Cool for 15 minutes before serving as the filling will be very hot.

COOK'S TIP
• If you like a sweeter pie, add 2–3 Tbsp sugar to the filling.

This dessert is not baklava, but it is inspired by the traditional Greek sweetmeat. Layers of filo are sandwiched around ice cream with honey and almonds roasted with cinnamon sugar.

LAURIE BLACK

Honey ice-cream 'baklava' with roasted almond crumbs

READY IN: 45 MINUTES
SERVES: 6

½ cup blanched almonds, roughly chopped
1 Tbsp sugar
1 tsp ground cinnamon
75g butter, melted
6 sheets filo pastry (see Glossary, page 172)
vanilla bean ice cream
liquid floral honey, at room temperature

1 Mix the almonds together with the sugar, cinnamon and 1 tsp melted butter. Spread the mix in a small roasting pan and bake at 180°C for 12 minutes, stirring every 4 minutes. Set the almond mix aside to cool.
2 Lie 1 sheet of filo out on a clean work surface, setting the remainder aside under a well-wrung out, damp, clean cloth. Brush the pastry sheet lightly with melted butter. Place another sheet on top and repeat, then another. Fold layered pastry in thirds lengthwise, then cut crosswise into 6 small sections. Brush the top of each section with a little more butter and transfer them to a baking tray lined with baking paper. Repeat the process with remaining 3 sheets of filo. Bake filo at 180°C for 9–12 minutes until golden. Set aside to cool.
3 To serve, place one section of filo on each plate and top with a spoonful of ice cream. Spoon some honey over the ice cream and sprinkle with some toasted almonds. Place another filo section on top and add a little more honey and sprinkle again with nuts. Serve immediately.

COOK'S TIP
• This is especially good made with thistle honey that is light in colour and not too sweet.

These cute little pastry and custard pies can be served with cream and fresh fruit.

TRACEY SUNDERLAND

Little Greek custard pies

READY IN: 45 MINUTES
SERVES: 4

2 cups (500ml) blue-top milk
peel of 1 lemon, in large pieces
¼ cup + 2 Tbsp semolina
2 eggs
½ cup sugar
1 tsp vanilla
6 sheets (130g) filo pastry (see Glossary, page 172)
3 Tbsp butter, melted
cinnamon and icing sugar, mixed
fresh cream and fruit, to serve

1 Put milk and pieces of lemon peel in a saucepan and bring to the boil. Once it has come to the boil, remove the peel, sprinkle in the semolina and stir until the mixture thickens a little.
2 In a separate bowl, beat eggs, sugar and vanilla together until creamy. Add this mix to the milk and semolina then stir over a low heat until thick. Remove from the heat and place plastic wrap over the custard to keep a skin from forming.
3 On a large board, lay out 1 sheet of filo pastry and brush generously with butter, cover with another sheet and repeat until you have 3 sheets. Cut the pastry into 4 even rectangles, spoon 2 Tbsp of custard into the middle of each pastry rectangle and fold into parcels. Repeat with the remaining sheets until you have 8 parcels.
4 Brush with remaining butter. Place pies, seam side down, on an oven tray. Bake at 180°C for 18–20 minutes or until golden.
5 Sprinkle each pie with the cinnamon and icing sugar mix. Serve with fresh cream and your choice of fruit.

COOK'S TIP
• Filo pastry will keep for up to 2 weeks in the fridge if wrapped tightly in plastic wrap then put back in a plastic bag and sealed well.

Low in fat and with a refreshing tang, this ice is ideal to serve in cones or piled high in tall glasses with fresh fruit, such as pawpaw or melon balls.

ALLYSON GOFTON

Pineapple & passionfruit ice

READY IN: 2 HOURS WITH ICE CREAM MAKER, 6–7 HOURS WITHOUT
MAKES: 7 CUPS

- 1 fresh tropical gold pineapple (4–5 cups fresh pineapple chunks)
- ¼ cup passionfruit pulp
- 2 cups plain unsweetened yoghurt
- 1 cup liquid glucose (see Cook's Tip)

1 Cut pineapple into chunks and process in a food processor until finely chopped.
2 Add the passionfruit pulp, yoghurt and glucose. Process until the mixture is well blended.
3 Freeze the mixture in an ice-cream maker according to the manufacturer's instructions and then transfer to a freezer-proof container. Place a piece of plastic film over the ice cream, to prevent ice crystals forming, before putting on the lid. Store in the freezer.
4 If not using an ice-cream maker, place the mixture in a metal baking pan, cover with plastic film and freeze for about 2 hours, until the mixture is softly set.
5 Return the mixture to the food processor and mix for 10–15 seconds until smooth and fluffy. Place the mixture back in the baking pan and freeze until half set. Process again and then transfer to a plastic container. Place a piece of plastic film on the surface of the ice-cream mixture, cover with the container lid and freeze for approximately 4 hours until solid. Use within 10 days.

COOK'S TIP

- Liquid glucose is sold in pharmacies and specialty food shops, such as Zarbo in Auckland (www.zarbo.co.nz). If you can't find any, use corn syrup.

This dessert is perfect with a little glass of dessert wine and can also be made with white-fleshed nectarines or fresh mangoes.

TRACEY SUNDERLAND

Caramelised nectarines with lime & mascarpone

READY IN: 20 MINUTES
SERVES: 4-6

- 6 ripe nectarines
- zest and juice of 3 limes
- 1 cup brown sugar
- 2 Tbsp butter
- 250g mascarpone, to serve

1 Wash nectarines, cut in half, remove stone and place in a shallow dish.

2 Sprinkle the lime zest and juice over the fruit. Cover in brown sugar and use your fingers to toss the nectarines in this syrup. Leave for a few minutes while the barbecue is heating.

3 Melt the butter on the preheated barbecue hotplate and immediately place the nectarines cut-side down on the plate. Tip a little syrup over the nectarines as they cook; they will need about 1-2 minutes on each side to turn golden. Return to the shallow dish and let them sit in the syrup.

4 Serve 2-3 nectarine halves per person with a spoonful of mascarpone and a little syrup spooned over.

COOK'S TIP

- To clean the barbecue after this sweet concoction, turn the gas to low and pour on a jug of water, scrape off the sugar and burnt pieces with a fish slice, then wipe with a thick layer of paper towels. Repeat until it's clean and rub a little oil back into the plate once it has cooled to stop it from rusting.

Serve this tangy and decadent, yet fuss-free, cheesecake with chargrilled limes.

TRACEY SUNDERLAND

Margarita cheesecake

READY IN: 2 HOURS
SERVES: 6–8

Cheesecake
250g plain biscuits, such as Round Wine
125g butter, melted
250g cream cheese
½ cup + 1 Tbsp sugar
2 eggs
165ml cream
150g natural sweetened yoghurt
100g limes
1 Tbsp tequila or brandy
1 Tbsp Grand Marnier liqueur or orange essence
15g gelatine

Chargrilled limes
1 Tbsp butter
4 limes, cut in half

To decorate
4 passionfruit
white chocolate shavings

1 Pulse the biscuits to a fine crumb in a food processor. Add butter and mix well. Tip into a greased 22cm-diameter tin with a removable base. Press evenly into the base and set aside.
2 Place the cream cheese into the bowl of a cake mixer and mix on low until smooth. Add the sugar and then the eggs, one by one. Beat until combined: it should be smooth, soft and fluffy.
3 Whip the cream to soft peaks. Do not over whip or it will be difficult to fold into the cheese mixture. Fold a ⅓ of the cream through the mixture then gently fold in remaining cream and the yoghurt.
4 Finely grate the limes and place the zest in a small ceramic bowl. Squeeze all the lime juice over the zest, add tequila and Grand Marnier and stir. Cover with plastic wrap and heat in the microwave for 40–50 seconds on high until boiling. Sprinkle the gelatine over and stir in quickly until it dissolves. If the mixture looks a little grainy, quickly reheat for 5–10 seconds.
5 Add a little of the cream cheese mixture to the gelatine liquid and mix well. Add this to the rest of the cheesecake mix and fold through evenly using a whisk.
6 Pour the mix over the prepared base and place in the coolest part of the refrigerator. Chill for at least 1½ hours.
7 To remove the cheesecake from the tin easily, run a warmed cloth slowly around the edge of the tin. The cheesecake will pull away from the sides. Use a fish slice to transfer the cheesecake to a serving plate. Cover with passionfruit pulp and white chocolate shavings.
8 To chargrill limes, heat a chargrill pan or frying pan over a high heat. Add butter then limes cut-side down. Sear for 3–5 minutes until the limes caramelise and turn golden. Remove and allow to cool.

This requires lashings of cream or ice cream to accompany it to make a really yummy family dessert.

ALLYSON GOFTON

Chocolate self-saucing pudding

READY IN: 1 HOUR
SERVES: 4–5

Pudding
1½ cups self-raising flour
2 Tbsp cocoa
100g butter
½ cup sugar
1 egg, beaten
1 cup milk
1 tsp vanilla essence

Sauce
2 Tbsp cocoa
½ cup sugar
2 cups boiling water

1 Sift the flour and cocoa into a bowl. Rub in the butter until the mixture resembles fine crumbs. Stir in the sugar and make a well in the centre.
2 Beat the egg, milk and vanilla essence together and mix into the dry ingredients with a holed spoon to form a stiff mixture. Turn the mixture into a greased 6-cup capacity ovenproof dish.
3 Mix the sauce ingredients together and pour over the batter.
4 Bake at 180°C for 45 minutes or until cooked. Serve hot with lashings of whipped cream.

COOK'S TIPS
• If you do not have an egg in the house, or you have a family member with an egg allergy, the egg can be omitted — just add an extra 3 Tbsp milk.
• For people who do not, or cannot, drink milk, this pudding will still work wonderfully using water as a substitute.

Truly worth a 'decadent-beyond-decadent' rating, this tart looks divine topped with berries or other seasonal fruit and served with a bowl of cream.

ALLYSON GOFTON

Chocolate mud tart

READY IN: 1–1½ HOURS
SERVES: 8

2 sheets pre-rolled butter pastry

Filling
100g butter, preferably unsalted, roughly chopped
275g dark chocolate, roughly chopped
½ cup cream
½ cup brown sugar
3 eggs
¾ cup ground almonds
berries, to decorate

1 Place the pastry sheets one on top of the other and roll out together to line the base and sides of a 24cm loose-bottom flan tin. Prick the flan base with a fork. Line with baking paper and fill with baking blind material (see Glossary, page 172). Bake at 190°C for about 12–15 minutes, or until the edges of the pastry are beginning to brown. Remove the baking blind material and return the flan to the oven for a further 2–3 minutes, or until the pastry is cooked in the centre. Set aside.
2 For the filling, put the butter, chocolate, cream and half the brown sugar in a double saucepan. Allow to melt over a moderate heat and stir until cool.
3 Beat together the eggs and remaining brown sugar for 2 minutes until lightly frothy. Whisk into the cooled chocolate mixture. Fold through the ground almonds and pour the filling into the prepared flan tin.
4 Bake on a pre-heated oven tray at 180°C for 30–35 minutes, or until the tart is set.
5 Remove from the oven and allow to cool before refrigerating for 2 hours. If refrigerating longer than this, have the tart at room temperature for 1 hour before serving.

COOK'S TIPS
• To gauge the quality of chocolate, check the label for cocoa solids — the higher the percentage of cocoa solids, the richer the flavour, the darker the colour and the glossier the finish will be.
• Use the finest chocolate you can afford here for the best flavour.

This is my mum's basic steamed pudding recipe, crowned with glacé apricots or peaches and studded with glacé ginger. Serve hot, hot, hot, with lashings of pouring cream.

ALLYSON GOFTON

Golden syrup ginger pudding

READY IN: 1½ HOURS
SERVES: 6-8

- 3-4 Tbsp golden syrup
- 200g glacé apricots or peaches
- ¼ cup crystallised ginger, chopped (plus ¼ cup extra if using on base, optional)
- 75g butter
- ¾ cup sugar
- 2 eggs
- 1½ cups flour
- 2 tsp baking powder
- ¾ cup milk
- 1 tsp ground ginger

1 Grease the base and sides of a 5 to 6-cup capacity pudding bowl. Spoon the golden syrup into the base and arrange glacé apricots or peaches over. Add ¼ cup chopped crystallised ginger to the fruit base, if using.

2 In a separate bowl beat the butter and sugar together until creamy. Add the eggs and beat well.

3 Sift together flour and baking powder. Stir into creamed mixture alternately with the milk. Fold in ¼ cup chopped ginger. Spoon the batter on top of the golden syrup and fruit. Cover with two layers of greaseproof paper and one of foil and secure tightly with string.

4 Place on a trivet or upside-down, old saucer in a large saucepan of boiling water. The water should come about ¾ of the way up the sides of the pudding bowl. Cover with the saucepan lid and simmer for 1¼ hours. Top the water level up with boiling water as it drops during cooking time.

5 Remove carefully from the heat. Stand 1-2 minutes then turn out onto a plate to serve. If wished, spoon extra golden syrup over the top.

COOK'S TIPS
• To cook in a microwave, grease the base and sides of a 5 to 6-cup capacity microwave-proof bowl. Spoon in 1 level Tbsp golden syrup and arrange the fruit as before. Fill with the pudding batter. There is no need to cover. Cook on high power (100 per cent) for 2 minutes, then cook on medium power (50 per cent) for 10 minutes. (Times are for a 900W microwave.) Stand 1 minute before turning out onto a serving plate. Pour remaining golden syrup over the top before serving.
• To cook in an oven, grease a 20cm-diameter cake tin and line with baking paper to come halfway up the sides of the tin. Spread the golden syrup over the base of the paper and arrange the fruit on the base. Top with the batter. Bake at 180°C for 40 minutes, or until a cake skewer inserted in the centre comes out clean. Stand 1-2 minutes before turning out upside down onto a cake plate to serve.

glossary

BAKING BLIND
Partially or fully baking a pastry case to ensure a crisp base, whether filling with a liquid ingredient or one that needs no further baking. Pastry is pricked with a fork, lined with baking paper and filled with dried beans, rice or special weights before baking.

BLACK OLIVE PASTE
Made of black olive flesh puréed with a little olive oil, it may be substituted with finely puréed tapenade (a rough or smooth purée of black olives with olive oil, garlic, capers, anchovy and sometimes rosemary). Available in jars at some supermarkets and deli counters.

COURT BOUILLON
Seasoned stock used for poaching fish, meat or vegetables.

DEEP-FRIED SHALLOTS
Used as a garnish, these shallots add a sweet and crunchy note to Asian dishes. Available in packets from Asian food stores or the Asian section of the supermarket.

DUKKAH
A coarse, dry mixture of coriander, cumin and sesame seeds, and hazelnuts that have been roasted separartely and lightly crushed together and seasoned with salt and pepper. Variations might include cinnamon, thyme, mint, oregano and pistachio nuts.

FILO PASTRY
Also called phyllo or strudel pastry, filo pastry is wafer thin, layered with melted butter and used to make pies or tarts, both sweet and savoury. The dough, made with strong flour (high in gluten) and only a little fat, is worked very hard to develop the gluten so the dough can be stretched or rolled out wafer thin. It's easier to buy filo pastry. You'll find it in the freezer or chiller at the supermarket.

HOT SMOKING
Involves preliminary cold smoking at around 10–30°C, then the temperature is raised and the food briefly hot smoked. The low smoking temperature ensures the smoke has time to permeate the fish, flavouring it, and with sufficient moisture-loss, extending the keeping time. The final blast of heat forms a skin and improves the colour, as well as enhancing the surface flavour.

KAFFIR LIME LEAVES
Glossy green bi-lobal leaves that bring a fresh lime scent to Asian dishes. Can be added whole to flavour stocks or rice, or torn or shredded (the tough mid-rib removed) for soups, sauces and marinades. Used raw in Vietnamese and Thai salads. Whole leaves can be used to wrap and flavour prawns, firm fish or chicken for barbecuing but, being very tough, they are removed before eating. Available from Asian foodstores and some larger supermarkets, or substitute with lemon leaves.

KIRSCH
A clear and dry brandy distilled from whole cherries, not to be confused with crème de kirsch, which is a sweet cherry liqueur.

PALM SUGAR
With deep brown to soft honey hues, warm caramel flavours and a fudge-like texture, palm sugar is palm tree sap that has been boiled to 'fudge' and set in moulds. Grate or crumble to use. Store in an airtight container so it does not become too brittle. Available from Asian food stores.

QUENELLES
Oval, poached dumplings, often of fish or meat, bound with egg and fat. Quenelles get their oval form when the mix is shaped between two spoons. Often the term is used loosely to describe the shape of a food rather than the process.

SCALOPPINE
(Or escalopes) Slices of meat pounded to make thin and tender.

SCORING SQUID
To prepare baby squid, cut along the natural groove and open flat. Wipe dry with a paper towel, score in criss-cross fashion and cut in half. Alternatively, you can cut squid tubes into thick rings.

SHAO HSING RICE WINE
The Shao Hsing brand is a good choice where rice wine is called for. It is made from glutinous rice and is used in Asian marinades and when stir-frying. Available from Asian grocery stores. Medium or dry sherry can be substituted for rice wine.

SNOW BEANS
A new hybrid vegetable, a cross between a snow pea and a flat runner bean, snow beans are best blanched and all parts are edible. Available from specialty fruit and vegetable stores.

THAI BASIL
A common herb in food from Thailand, Vietnam, Laos and Cambodia. The leaves are deep green, while flowers, buds and stems are purplish. It has a sweet licorice, aniseedy taste and is available in Asian stores, some supermarkets and greengrocers, or can be grown in a herb garden.

VERJUICE
Usually the fermented juice of unripe grapes, verjuice can be made from other fruit. It has a lemon-like tartness with the tang of vinegar, but is milder than both. Good for adding a lift to sauces and soups, casseroles and sautés and to deglaze frying pans and roasting dishes, especially after cooking chicken, turkey or fish. Available from supermarkets.

index

baked savoury cheesecake — 10
baking
   Barbados gingerbread — 146
   basic one-rise bread — 122
   blueberry turnovers — 144
   brown-sugar shortbread — 124
   citrus & almond cake — 120
   gruyère & pecan scones — 128
   hazelnut biscuits — 132
   Mum's tea cake — 126
   small apple cinnamon turnovers — 142
   super-duper Louise cake — 130
   toll house biscuits — 138
   white chocolate brownies — 140
beef
   beef & bean chilli with avocado salsa — 76
   sage & peppered scotch fillet with fresh cream sauce — 82
beetroot, apple & blue cheese salad with walnut cider dressing — 28
blueberry turnovers — 144
bread, basic one-rise — 122
broad bean & mint dip — 98

caramelised nectarines with lime & mascarpone — 162
ceviche, snapper & shrimp — 106
cherry & apple pie — 154
chicken
   chicken & chilli enchiladas — 74
   chicken noodle salad — 14
   chicken steaks with green olive salsa — 68
   chicken, spinach & mushroom tart — 56
   kaffir lime chicken kebabs — 94
   parmesan crumbed chicken scallopine with polenta — 58
   prosciutto chicken wraps with chunky oven chips — 64
chocolate mud tart — 168

chocolate self-saucing pudding — 166
citrus & almond cake — 120
curry puff pies — 12

desserts
   caramelised nectarines with lime & mascarpone — 162
   cherry & apple pie — 154
   chocolate mud tart — 168
   chocolate self-saucing pudding — 166
   golden syrup ginger pudding — 170
   honey ice-cream 'baklava' with roasted almond crumbs — 156
   little Greek custard pies — 158
   little lime curd meringue tarts — 136
   margarita cheesecake — 164
   pineapple & passionfruit ice — 160
   rose & raspberry meringues with cream — 150
   summer pudding — 152
dips
   broad bean & mint dip — 98
   guacamole — 114
   mint dip — 100
   minted sour cream dip — 116
   sour cream, salmon & lime dip — 98
   tomato & lime dip — 110
dressings
   garlic mayo — 42
   sweet onion dressing — 44
   tuna mayonnaise — 104
   walnut cider dressing — 28
   yoghurt dressing — 48
drunken pork chops — 40

field mushroom cannelloni — 62
fish
   fish pie with spring onion mash — 50
   fish wrapped in vine leaves with tzatziki — 90

   hot-smoked salmon summer salad with fresh garlic mayo — 42
   lemon & pepper salmon with béarnaise sauce — 84
   pan-fried fish with lemon, caper & parsley sauce — 52
   smoked fish, lemon, parsley & celery-heart salad — 26
   snapper & shrimp ceviche — 106
four-cheese baked macaroni — 70
fritters
   gruyère fritters, salad greens & sweet onion dressing — 44
   wood-smoked mussel & zucchini fritters — 60

goat's feta & smoked bacon, brown bread sandwiches — 18
golden syrup ginger pudding — 170
green lip mussels with fresh herbs & pasta — 72
green velvet soup — 16
gruyère & pecan scones — 128
gruyère fritters, salad greens & sweet onion dressing — 44
guacamole — 114

hazelnut biscuits — 132
herb-scented barbecued lamb with olive paste & skordalia — 93
honey ice-cream 'baklava' with roasted almond crumbs — 156
hot-smoked salmon summer salad with fresh garlic mayo — 42

Indian-spiked potato kebabs with tomato & lime dip — 110

kaffir lime chicken kebabs — 94

lamb
   lamb & cashew curry 38
   lamb burgers with roast
     peppers & fried onion 66
   herb-scented barbecued
     lamb with olive paste &
     skordalia 93
   perfect roast lamb 88
Laurie's lemon curd 134
lemon & pepper salmon
   with béarnaise sauce 84
lime curd 134, 136
little Greek custard pies 158
little lamb pies with rosemary,
   chilli & tomato 24
little lime curd meringue tarts 136

margarita cheesecake 164
Mexican albondigas soup with
   limes & soft tortillas 30
Mum's tea cake 126
mushrooms on toast with
   soft onions, sherry & capers 54

orange curd 134
oven chips, chunky 64

pakoras with mint dip 100
pan-fried fish with lemon,
   caper & parsley sauce 52
parsley sauce 52
passionfruit curd 134
pasta
   field mushroom cannelloni 62
   four-cheese baked macaroni 70
   green lip mussels with fresh
     herbs & pasta 72
   spinach & ham lasagne 70
perfect roast lamb 88
pies
   cherry & apple pie 154
   curry puff pies 12
   fish pie with spring

     onion mash 50
   little Greek custard pies 158
   little lamb pies with
     rosemary, chilli & tomato 24
   picnic pie of ham, egg &
     roasted tomato 34
small apple cinnamon
   turnovers 142
pineapple & passionfruit ice 160
pita filled with grilled eggplant,
   yoghurt, dukkah & coriander 20
potato & smoked cheese
   quesadillas 112
potato cream soup 18
pork
   drunken pork chops 40
   roast pork with dried blueberry
     & nut stuffing 80
   tossed pork & garlic chives
     in cos cups 46
   prosciutto chicken wraps with
     chunky oven chips 64

raspberry curd 134
refired-bean nachos with
   guacamole 114
roast pork with dried blueberry
   & nut stuffing 80
rose & raspberry meringues
   with cream 150

sage & peppered scotch fillet
   with fresh cream sauce 82
salads
   beetroot, apple & blue cheese
     salad with walnut cider dressing 28
   chicken noodle salad 14
   hot-smoked salmon summer
     salad with fresh garlic mayo 42
   smoked fish, lemon, parsley
     & celery-heart salad 26
   yoghurt-dressed roast lamb,
     potato & mint salad 48
salsa, avocado 76

salsa, green olive 68
salt & pepper chilli prawns
   & squid 86
samosa pastry 12
sauce
   béarnaise sauce 52
   béchamel sauce 70
   fresh cream sauce (savoury) 82
   parsley sauce 52
sausages in red wine with
   red onion, rosemary
   & parsley 108
scotch fillet, sage & peppered
   with fresh cream sauce 82
skordalia 92
small apple cinnamon turnovers 142
smoked fish, lemon, parsley
   & celery-heart salad 26
smoked paprika & prawn
   tramezzini 102
snapper & shrimp ceviche 106
soup
   green velvet soup 16
   Mexican albondigas soup 30
   potato cream soup 18
sour cream, salmon & lime dip 98
spinach & ham lasagne 36
spring onion mash 50
summer pudding 152
super-duper Louise cake 130

Thai-spiced pumpkin chips
   with minted sour cream 116
toll house biscuits 138
tossed pork & garlic chives
   in cos cups 46
tzatziki 90

vitello tonnato 104

white chocolate brownies 140
wood-smoked mussel
   & zucchini fritters 60

author profiles

Allyson Gofton trained as a chef and has been writing for New Zealand home cooks since 1983. She has penned 17 cookbooks and for the last 10 years has presented the highly successful *Food in a Minute* TV segment. However, the job she loves most is writing as a food editor for *Taste* and *Next* magazines, closely followed by reading about food history.

Jennifer Yee is a food design and nutrition consultant with more than 18 years' experience in the food industry. Her two highly regarded books, *Discovering Asian Ingredients* and the award-winning *Chow Down & Chill Out — fast Asian recipes for busy people,* have become essentials for everyone who likes Asian food. Jennifer is a regular contributor to *Taste* magazine.

Laurie Black is food editor for both *Taste* and Auckland's *Metro* magazine, which means she does a lot of investigative shopping, sampling and eating out in the course of her work. She has nine years' experience as a food writer and has an enduring respect for classic cooking, while delighting in the new.

Tracey Sunderland is a chef with many years' overseas experience. Whipping up recipes while juggling family life, Tracey is now dedicated to designing food that complements a busy lifestyle. She joined *Taste* as a food writer on the launch of the magazine and every month writes a midweek meals feature delivering accessible, quickly made yet delicious recipes.